D0211642

The Throwaway Kids

The Throwaway Kids

Dr. Gary Simpkins

BROOKLINE BOOKS • BROOKLINE, MASSACHUSETTS

LC 2778
.R4
S56
2002

.i 12191553

49902830

Copyright 2002 by Brookline Books

All rights reserved. No part of this work may be reproduced or transmitted in any form or by any means, electronic or mechanical, including photocopying and recording, or by any information storage or retrieval system, without permission in writing from the publisher.

ISBN 1-57129-091-5

Library of Congress Cataloging-in-Publication Data

Simpkins, Gary.
        The throwaway kids / by Gary Simpkins.
            p. cm.
    Includes bibliographical references.
        ISBN 1-57129-091-5 (pbk.)
    1. African American teenagers--Education. 2. African American teenagers--Language. 3. Reading. 4. Black English. 5. Language and education--United States. I. Title: Throwaway kids. II. Title.
        LC2778.R4 S56 2002
        373.182996'073--dc21

                                    2002008660

Printed in the USA
10 9 8 7 6 5 4 3
Cover by Nathan Budoff
Published by
Brookline Books
P.O. Box 97
Newton Upper Falls, MA 02464
1-800-666-BOOK

Acknowledgements

To Milton Budoff, Ph.D. for his editorial assistance, encouragement, and guidance.

To Patricia Young, Ph.D. for her insightful and invaluable in-depth analysis of the *Bridge* reading program.

To Charlesetta Stalling for use of data from her study on the cultural context of reading and her review of the literature.

Contents

Preface

It has been a gratifying intellectual experience watching Dr. Gary Simpkins develop his Associative Bridge Reading Program over the past twenty years. He took on a very difficult task of dealing with both a neglected area (the failure of Black children to read) and a topic that has been rejected by the scholarly community (using Ebonics as a bridge to teach reading). Dr. Simpkins begins his monograph with the compelling and cogent observation, "There is a crisis brewing in this country's public school system: the continuing patterns of long-term failure of Black urban students who are culturally different." It takes not only ability but also downright courage to develop materials in an area, which itself has been so controversial and rejected. Yet, Dr. Simpkins is unique in offering teachers and reading specialists a field-validated approach that offers hope to Black children.

On September 11, 2001, this nation was shocked by the terrorist attack on the World Trade Center of New York City and the Pentagon in Washington, DC. A headline in a local newspaper read:

> September 11 attacks change class curriculums. Instructors are revamping their curriculums to account for recent terrorist attacks.
> — *Columbia Missourian, October 17, 2001 p. 2*

This terrorist attack, indeed, was a national tragedy unheard of in the history of this country. Yet there are other tragedies occurring daily in this country, tragedies that never get the headline attention the terrorist attacks received, and never inspire curriculum changes. Yes, the September attacks, they say, changed this country. But it did not change for millions of Black children trapped in the educational system who wind up as dropouts or are misplaced in special education classes. Business goes on as usual. These academic tragedies are referred to by Dr. Simpkins in this book, *The Throwaway Kids*.

Who are these "throwaway kids"? Simpkins is talking about the extremely high dropout—or pushout—rate of Black children in U.S. schools. In a St. Louis high school, for example, 500 Black students entered a local high school in ninth grade. Of that number, only 105 (21%) graduated. If 79% of airplanes crashed in a four year period of time, the airline industry would be in serious trouble. Black kids are falling out of public schools all over the country as 'throwaway' problems. And who really cares about these throwaway kids? What happens to them? Many will end up as a statistic: unemployed, in jail, dead, on drugs, or alcoholic.

It is no accident that one out of every four Black males is either incarcerated or monitored in some way by the criminal justice system. Further, it is no accident that over 50% of African American males under 21 are unemployed. A prediction was made that, if current trends continue, by the year 2020, 70% of Black males will be unemployed, in jail, dead, on drugs, or alcoholic. These are the victims that Dr. Simpkins calls the throwaways.

A major feature of *Throwaway Kids* is a research-based method for teaching children to read, thus potentially saving millions. Linguists and educators have evaluated the Associative Bridging teaching technique and found it effective in improving reading skills. The Bridge method takes John Dewey's philosophy of "Begin where the child is" as a starting point. Consequently, Simpkins uses the child's language as the point of departure for the reading program. The program is divided into three sections. The stories that form the backbone of the reading materials are written first in language that is familiar to the child—the child's home language, Ebonics. A second version of the story is written 50% in the child's home language and 50% in semi-familiar Standard English. The same story is written a third time completely in Standard English.

Simpkins uses an important process of peer control and student oral feedback to give the non-mainstream child control over the learning process. This is an important variable particularly as these children begin to experience control over their academic fate. As Dr. Simpkins argues, it is very important for the Black child to feel inner-directed and "in charge" of the learning process.

The first section of Throwaway Kids reviews the public schools' failure to educate the Black child, particularly how the Black child has been mis-educated or dis-educated. Clearly, then, Black children are in need of new teaching models that can provide positive educational experiences. As the late Dr. Bobby Wright stated, mis-education leads to a process he called "mentacide", the systematic and deliberate destruction of a group's mind.

The essence of how to prevent throwaway children is contained in the second part of the book. Simpkins presents the Associative Bridge method as a solution to teaching Black children to read. This method has two components, a) the development of instructional materials that reflect Black language and culture, and b) the development of instructional materials that reflect mainstream/non-mainstream language and culture. Dr. Simpkin's book is very timely in view of the new thrust in Washington on revamping the educational system.

In his testimony before the House Committee on Education, Secretary of Education Dr. Paige recently stated the following plan of the Bush Administration:

> President Bush made education his highest priority and laid out his education agenda, called "No Child Left Behind"...For minority students, misclassification or inappropriate placement in special education

programs can have significant adverse consequences, particularly when these students are being removed from regular education settings and denied access to the core curriculum...President Bush means "No Child Left Behind" literally...(he) means that all of our kids, even the ones the system calls 'hard to teach', can learn. He understands that children with disabilities are most likely to be left behind and have been historically left out and left behind.

— *The Challenger, November 8-14, 2001, p. 2*

"Being left behind" is another way of saying that these children will, to use Simpkins' terminology, become throwaways. To be sure, it is only a matter of time that the ones left behind will be the ones who drop out or are pushed out.

What happens to the child who by fate is *not* left behind and does *not* become a throwaway? An example of the famous Dr. Ben Carson will illustrate.

Beating the Odds

A television special on the Johns Hopkins Medical Center in Baltimore, Maryland gave many of us an opportunity to see one of our Black heroes who might have become a Throwaway. He is the gifted surgeon, Dr. Ben Carson, Director of the Division of Pediatric Neurosurgery and Professor of Neurosurgery, Oncology, Plastic Surgery, and Pediatrics at Johns Hopkins.

Dr. Carson is world famous for his skill in performing complicated surgeries on children with brain and spinal cord injuries. He first gained worldwide recognition in 1987 when he became the first surgeon, Black or White, to successfully separate Siamese twins joined at the back of the head. Both twins survived, following a procedure that took five months to plan and 22 hours to perform. Incredible as it may seem, Dr. Carson was almost a throwaway. He overcame adversity and beat the odds.

Dr. Carson was such a poor student in elementary school that his fifth-grade classmate nicknamed him "Dummy". He got into fights over whether he was just "the dumbest kid in the class" or "the dumbest person in the world." At that point of his life, he was completely unmotivated by failing grades, low self-esteem and a terrible temper. By all measures, he was a child in danger of being left behind.

Fortunately Dr. Carson had two things working in his favor. One was a strong faith in God that continues to sustain him. The other was a mother who was involved in his life and continued to believe in him. Ms. Carson was a single parent who prayed her son would go beyond her third-grade education. Consequently, she sent her son to the public library everyday instead of letting him play outdoors, watch television, or play video games. In addition, he had to read books and turn in two book reports to her every week. Initially, Dr. Carson thought this was a case of child abuse. But as he began to read, his entire world opened up.

Dr. Carson began to realize that through books and reading he could go anywhere and do anything. He became interested in learning and aspired to something more than the factory job and nice car that his classmates wanted. By seventh grade he was at the top of his class. His love of reading, learning and commitment to excellence and doing his best were fully ingrained. As he now says, "When I was in fifth grade, I thought I was stupid, so I conducted myself like a stupid person. When I was in seventh grade, I thought I was smart; I conducted myself like a smart person and achieved like a smart person." It was not until later that Dr. Carson realized his mother had not even been able to read the book reports that had turned his life around.

Eventually, Dr. Carson received a scholarship to Yale University and went on the medical school at the University of Michigan. By age 33 he had earned his current position at Johns Hopkins. Dr. Carson, the almost Throwaway Kid, has written three best-selling books, received more than 20 honorary degrees, 60 national citations of merit, and numerous honors and awards.

But that is not the end of the story. What about the single parent, Ms. Carson? Not only did Ms. Carson turn her son's life around, but also, she eventually taught herself to read, earned her G.E.D. and graduated from college. In 1994, she was awarded an honorary doctorate degree, making her Dr. Sonya Carson!

Dr. Ben Carson is exactly the kind of youth that Dr. Gary Simpkins has researched with his Associative Bridge reading program. His research clearly shows that a culture-specific approach proved more effective than traditional reading programs. The result is new sense of hope and motivation for Black children.

As we enter the 21st century, this nation cannot afford to leave undeveloped the talents of millions of children who happen to be born different by virtue of race, language, sex, income status or mental ability. Nor can this nation ignore, under the pretense of educational excellence, the unfinished national task of offering every child, Black, Hispanic, Native American, Asian and White, an equal chance to learn and become a self-sufficient and productive citizen. Education is a fundamental right deserving protection under the 14th Amendment, which guarantees all Americans equal protection under the law. This book will give new direction to all who are sincere about confronting and overcoming this enormous waste of human potential.

Robert L. Williams, Ph.D.
Distinguished Visiting Professor of Black Studies
The University of Missouri-Columbia

1

Introduction

There is a crisis brewing in this country's public school system: the consequences of the continuing long term failure of Black urban students who are culturally different. This impending crisis has the potential to impact the entire nation in terms of higher crime rates, escalated civil disobedience and dramatic increases in Black, culturally different students, also referred to as inner-city, culturally disadvantaged and culturally depressed. These students are in danger of being "given up on" by the public school system and the government. They are at risk of becoming 'public school throwaways.'

The term 'public school throwaways' can be defined as those students who are forced to drop out of school or are expelled due to their schools' inability to teach them to read in grade school and work with grade appropriate subject materials later. Their resulting frustration causes them to drop out of high school early, become alienated from society and commit crimes. These students and those older than them now account for the high juvenile and adult incarceration rates—one of four middle and late adolescents are involved with the criminal justice system. An enormous percentage of the convicts in prisons are illiterate.

Schools continue to fail them, which, along with other features of their lives, leads to their alienation and ongoing frustration.

For these students, school represents a continuous cycle of failure, frustration and humiliation.

Not only have the schools, in many cases, given up on these students ever learning as what they consider the expected rate for the normal child; all too often, very early in their academic careers, the students have given up on themselves (Kozol, 1968), These students, in order to boost their fragile, severely damaged academic egos, frequently engage in disruptive classroom behaviors. They often adopt an attitude of 'who needs school.'

It is not unusual for them to turn to gangs and groups whose value system is antagonistic towards school and society in search of the support and reinforcement they do not receive in school. Black public school students, according to Labov (1976), this author, and other researchers of inner-city children and youth, can be divided into two groups. One grouping can be labeled as Black mainstream; the other as Black non-mainstream students.

Black mainstream students are in large part members of the middle and upper socio-economic class. On the whole, they do not participate in the street culture or internalize its value system. They can be described as assimilated into the mainstream culture; in the process of being assimilated or striving to become assimilated.

Their language of choice is standard English. They often possess 'code switching' skills, the ability to switch from standard English to the vernacular language code. Doing well in school is important to them, their reading scores tend to be on the average one or two grades behind the national norm. They are increasing their scores and progress in learning is taking place.

The majority of Black students belong to the Black non-mainstream grouping. The term "Black non-mainstream" refers to African American students who are generally members of the lower socio-economic class. They speak what has become known as African American Language, Black Dialect, African American Vernacular English or Ebonics, and relate to the larger culture as a value system which their language population represents. In the social science literature they are described as 'disadvantaged', 'inner-city' and other labels mentioned in this chapter and Chapter 4.

Their patterns of reading and academic achievement in the schools are quite different from the mainstream Black students. These students' reading scores reach a ceiling at the reading level of grade 4.9 and persist there through grades 11 and 12 .

Despite the fact that verbal skills in their vernacular culture are highly prized and reinforced, these students, unlike their white counterparts, demonstrate no correlation between their individual verbal skills and their reading scores.

Among students in this grouping, the most endangered, the most at risk, are adolescents who have been promoted from elementary school to middle school without having acquired adequate reading skills. Many of these students have failed or received D- grades in all of their courses with the possible exception of shop courses and physical education, but were continually promoted based solely on their age.

By the time students get to the third or fourth grade they are expected to read independently and to have mastered most of the basic reading skills. Once a student progresses to middle school, reading is no longer a part of the curriculum. It is assumed that the students possess the functional reading skills necessary to navigate their way through the subject matters taught there.

For the majority of Black non-mainstream students this assumption does not hold true. These students are not only deficient in their ability to read and understand age and grade appropriate materials, they have great difficulty with the entire range of academic subject matter. The term 'functionally illiterate' best describes these students.

Their problem (school related failure) is so enormous that many of these students give up before reaching the fourth grade.

This occurs in spite of the fact that as preschoolers they looked forward to attending school and entered school happy and excited about learning.

If these students learn to cope with the frustration of failure, and remain in school, i.e. they do not dropout or get expelled, they often receive a high school diploma. This occurs even though, they are, in the truest sense of the term, functionally illiterate.

This gives rise to the question "How is this possible?" The answer is "social promotion", a term few parents are familiar with. In the 1970's schools in this country began a policy of promoting students based on age. Although the term 'social promotion' came into existence in the 70's the practice existed in many schools long before it was labeled.

In recent years educators and politicians have become strongly opposed to this practice. Former President Clinton, in a memorandum to the Secretary of Education, stated that he had "repeatedly challenged states and school districts to end social promotion. To require students to meet rigorous academic standards at key transition points in their schooling careers, and to end the practice of promoting students without regard to how much they have learned... Students should not be promoted past the fourth grade if they cannot read independently and well, and should not enter high school without a solid foundation."

President Clinton's proposal to create voluntary national tests in the areas of reading and math stirred interest in the Congress and in the educational community on the use of testing to evaluate schools' performance. The former president called for "appropriate use of test and other indicators of academic performance in determining whether students should be promoted."

In advocating testing to end social promotions and to add accountability to education, Clinton is by no means alone. Newly elected President George Bush, when Governor of Texas, was one of the nation's strongest advocates of testing in the public schools and has pursued this agenda in the Congress during this first year of his term. In New York City the Chancellor proposed that students in the 4th and 7th grades be held back if they failed to pass the state's reading test at these grade levels.

States and school districts are not just debating and proposing test based requirements for promotion and retention, they are in the process of actually implementing them. In 1997, according to the American Federation of Teachers, 46 states had, or were in the process of developing or reviewing assessment devices for promotion and retention.

Social promotion appears to be on the way out of the American public school systems. If progress continues at the current rate, in the next several years, social promotion will be a thing of the past. But there is a dark down side to the demise of social promotion and the current enthusiasm for the use of achievement tests.

There exists a growing body of research evidence which indicates that grade retention, in general, has no beneficial effect on students socially or academically. The students retained in the same grade not only failed to learn more than the students who were socially promoted, but suffered tremendous damage to their egos. They tended to believe that they were being punished because they were dumb, and as a result had higher dropout rates.

This seems to defy logic and common sense. If two students are failing a grade level and one repeats the grade while the other goes on to the next level, the one who is promoted is better off than the one who repeats the grade. To put it another way, does a student do better repeating a grade level he has failed or would he have done just as well, or better, if he had been promoted with his peers?

According to the research data repeating a grade does not generally improve academic achievement (Holmes 1998, House 1989). The data indicate that not only does the student repeating the grade not fare better academically, his chances of dropping out of school are greatly increased (Gampert and Opperman, 1988, Olson 1990, Anderson 1994, Reardon 1996).

Anderson, after conducting an extensive large scale study of the efforts of grade retention on drop out rates, found that students who were currently repeating a grade were 70% more likely to drop out of high school. Negative findings on the effects of retaining students in the same grade have also been reported by Grisson and Shepard (1987) and Luppiscu et al. (1995).

Over the past two decades there has been a trend toward extending kindergarten to two years for many children in America (with the largest percentage being minority students). This practice has various names: extended kindergarten, pre-first, transition and readiness rooms, junior-first grade.

According to Shepard (1991), such decisions are based on assumptions of immaturity or presumed academic deficiencies. The tests used to make readiness and retention decisions are inappropriately or technically inaccurate to justify such special placements. Such tests, called readiness tests, are in reality, thinly disguised IQ tests, referred to by the schools as developmental screening measures or academic skills tests.

These tests tend to identify a disproportionately large number of Black, culturally different children as unready for school. The tests ignore the fact that before the age of 7 or 8, standardized tests of achievement measures are psychometrically inappropriate for making decisions about individual children and school placements.

In the case of culturally different children, the problem appears to be that these tests tap knowledge that the children are assumed to have spontaneously acquired from their home environment.

It has been known for some time that Black children are not

achieving in this country's public school systems. It is documented in the literature that as Black children proceed through the school, they fall behind the national average at all grade levels, on all academic measures. The longer they are in school the further behind they fall. This phenomenon known as 'The Cumulative Deficit' was coined in the late fifties by Professor Benjamin Bloom. It came into fashion with the publication of the Coleman Report (1966).

The United States Commissioner of Education was directed by the Civil Rights Act of 1964 to conduct a study on the "lack of availability of equal educational opportunities" for minority groups. This study became the second largest of its kind in American history. The study tested 570,000 public school students. The report "Equality of Educational Opportunity," known as the Coleman Report after Dr. James Coleman who headed the study, was released two years later.

The Coleman Report, among other things, pointed out that minority schools were not particularly unequal. The data showed that neither teacher-pupil ratio or per-pupil expenditures showed any relationship to minority academic achievement. The findings of the study confounded the experts in educational social policy.

Congress, educational social policy makers, as well as the authors of the study, expected to find that minorities had unequal school facilities, resources, etc., which led to unequal school achievement. They also expected that the unequal resources and unequal school outcomes were mainly in the Southern states.

The Coleman Report data showed more than anything else, that minority students (mainly Blacks) were not, in a large part, benefitting from the public school system. The longer they stayed in school, the dumber they became, if one measures dumbness by the distance behind the national norms. The study also showed that this phenomenon, 'The Cumulative Deficit' was in no way unique to the Southern states. According to the study, it was definitely nationwide.

Unbelievable as it may seem, the Coleman Report was greeted with silence and indifference. Little concern was shown by the Department of Health, Education and Welfare, the professional education community, or the Black community's leadership organizations.

In 1969, under the leadership of Daniel P. Moynihan, later a senator from New York, and Thomas Pettegrew, a social psychology professor, a faculty seminar was organized at Harvard University to reexamine the data on which the Coleman Report findings were based. The group was composed of distinguished professors in and outside the field of education.

After three years of intensive study and analysis by the Harvard group, much of the original data was revised, but the primary conclusions remained the same. Black students were not substantially benefitting from attendance at public schools. The relative standing of Black students in relation to white students remained essentially constant in terms of standard deviations, but the absolute differences in terms of grade level discrepancies increased over time; the longer Black students stayed in school the further behind they slipped. The Harvard study findings and analysis were published in a book entitled *On Equality of Education of Opportunity* (Mostseller, F. and Moynihan, D.P.).

Among other things, the Coleman Report and the Harvard reexamination of the report showed that the American public school system was, for all intents and purposes, essentially a segregated system. Eighty percent of all white students in the first and the twelfth grades attended schools that were 90 to 100% white.

Since 1967, these numbers have increased. It can be said that America has a highly segregated system of public education which borders on being two separate systems. The reports found that two variables made a major difference for Black students: social class and 'sense of control of the environment'. The teacher's effect also made a difference, but it was extremely slight.

Socio-economic status was predictive of school outcomes because Black students who score high on these variables tend to have acquired more of the class values which the schools are based on, including language, culture, and interest. Although they still displayed features of the 'cumulative deficit', their school outcome measures were significantly higher than those of Black students in the lower socio-economic levels. Considering the school as a cultural entity, the closer the students are to the culture of the school, the greater their outcome score will be.

In the Coleman Report and the reexamination, of all the variables measured including all measures of family background, and all school and academic variables, one variable, sense of control of the environment, showed the strongest relationship to school achievement. Black students who had a strong sense of control of the environment scored better than white students with a weaker sense of control.

In this author's opinion, this finding, the sense of control of the environment, was the most significant finding of the Coleman Report and the Harvard reexamination. Both Coleman, et al., and the Harvard group 'missed the boat', however, when it came to understanding the importance of these variables. They failed to recognize what the 'sense of control of the environment' variable was measuring in Black students (especially Black non-mainstream students) and why it correlated so highly with school outcomes.

A number of the critics of the reports believed the sense of control variable pointed out the need for community control of the school and in part they were right. But the real significance of the findings had more to do with the exclusion and often antagonism shown toward the students' language and value system, family structure and overall culture.

The fact that the public school system is a product of mainstream society, designed by mainstream educators for mainstream students, was overlooked. The school system was designed to be the primary vehicle for socialization. It was believed to be a great 'melting pot' where culturally different students could shed their ethnic imperatives and blend into American society.

The problem was that for sizable numbers of Black students there was no melting pot. The students tenaciously held on to their language and culture. What was needed was a recipe for vegetable soup.

To further complicate things, it was believed by the mainstream (those in power) that non-mainstream students and their families had no culture, only a distorted version of white American culture. It therefore follows that having no culture of their own they could only be measured or judged by the degree to which they had acquired white mainstream culture.

Although not intentionally, the Coleman Report and the Harvard reexamination of the report provided fuel for what became known as the "Cultural Deficit Model." If the Black children's failure in the schools could not be explained by school conditions, it was reasoned that there were two alternative explanations, genetics or environment. The problem must reside in the students and their families' genetic makeup (low intelligence) or in the environment/culture of the students. These were the choices seen by the mostly liberal social science and academic establishment.

The choice of genetics was found to be distasteful. This left them with the task of looking at the students, their family structure, language and culture (environment) for the answers. Few scholars and educators, considered that the students' failure might not reside in the students' family culture, etc., but in institutional failure; the cause of the failure might reside in the school systems' inability to accommodate cultural differences among these students.

The Pressure for Standards on Black Non-mainstream Students

As stated earlier, most of the states in this country have in place or are in the process of implementing promotion/retention policies based primarily on standardized tests. While almost no one is in favor of social promotion, policymakers, educators and politicians are faced with a fundamental dilemma. With the increased pressure for standards, what will happen to Black non-mainstream students who are in the grasp of "the cumulative deficit"?

The number of Black students retained will dramatically increase. But when a student is retained one grade, the probability of dropping out of high school is increased by 80%. What will happen when these students are held back more than one grade? What will happen when these students come to believe they will never be able to graduate from high school?

There exists today a disproportionate number of African Americans interacting with the criminal justice system. It must be emphasized that this is a forced interaction. In 1991 African Americans accounted for 12.3% of the population nationwide and 43.4% of the inmate population in state prisons. While African Americans are 12.3% of the population they account for 31% of all arrests made and 40.8% of prisoners executed. According to Jones (1995) one out of every three Black men between the ages of 20 and 29 'were within the grasp' of the criminal justice system.

With the introduction of standardized tests mediating promotion and graduation nationally (all states if the Congress signs the education bill before them in 2001) something must be done to break the cycle of "the cumulative deficit". Otherwise, these figures, which this author finds appalling and clearly racist, will increase dramatically. The number of African Americans incarcerated will grow and the age level at which they come into the criminal justice system will decrease. Greater numbers of teens and preteens will be incarcerated.

According to Reseda high school Principal Robert Khadafa, the California high school exit exam will be "harder than the CBEST test, which teachers have to pass to become teachers."

The above mentioned, combined with the fact that the nation's schools have, at this time, no way, methods or means, to break the cycle of the cumulative deficit process makes for many potential tragedies. The policymaker's answer appears to be give the children more of what has failed them in the past. Which amounts to throwing the student away.

Nothing has changed since the 1966 release of the Coleman Report for Black non-mainstream students. It is as true today as it was in 1966: the longer Black students stay in the public schools the further behind the national norms they get.

Data presented before Senator Spector's U.S. Senate Ebonics panel in January, 1977 by Michael Casserly, Executive Director of the Council of Great City Schools, summarized the performance of students in 50 large urban public school districts, a sample which included hundreds of schools. The data clearly demonstrate that, while white students in these schools showed steady improvement in their reading achievement scores as they got older (60.7% read above the fiftieth percentile norm at the elementary school level in 1992-3, and 65.4 did so by high school), the opposite was true of African American students. These students showed a steady decline (31.3 % read above the fiftieth percentile norm at the elementary level, while only 26.6% did so by the time they got to high school.

Data from the 1999 National Association of Educational Progress, showed the same discouraging trend. On a 500 point scale, African American students by the age of nine, were an average of 29 points behind the scores of their white counterparts; by the age of 12 they were 31 points behind and by the age of 17 they were 37 points behind.

An article entitled "The Real Test" in the *New Republic* magazine reported on a plan proposed by President Bush to reform the American public schools.

> "All hail the new education consensus. That was the sentiment in Washington this week when President Bush unveiled his first major policy proposal, a 47.6 billion plan to reform America's schools. With its focus on helping poor minority children in the inner-city schools via a combination of increased spending, new testing, and tougher accountability, the plan was lauded by congressional Republicans and Democrats alike."

The prescription for achieving accountability is believed to be better school facilities, higher pay for teachers, smaller class size, after school programs and more rigorous standards as measured by standardized tests at various grade levels (if not all grade levels). In the plan, testing and tougher accountability are interchangeable.

How will these plans affect Black non-mainstream students when, at this time, social scientific and educational policy makers have demonstrated that they are totally impotent when it comes to breaking or even interrupting the "cumulative deficit" cycle for these students? What will happen when the students are held back more than one grade level? What will happen when they come to believe that they will never graduate from high school?

John R. Rickford, professor of linguistics at Stanford University, who has extensively researched the language culture and education of African Americans, offered the following useful comments. "...while I agree that the very best general principles of teaching and learning should be followed in the education of all students, the evidence that schools are failing massive numbers of

African American students with existing methods is so overwhelming that it would be counterproductive and offensive to continue using them uncritically." To turn the powerful words of the Reverend Jesse Jackson on their head, to accept existing methods represents "an unconditional surrender, bordering on a disgrace!"

The Proposal

What is needed is a new, creative solution, rather than spending billions of dollars giving the non-mainstreamed student more of the same old tired solutions which have not worked in the past. In the next chapters, we present arguments for curricula for Black non-mainstreamed adolescents that are based on their distinctive linguistic and cultural experience generally, and in relation to reading. We then describe the requirements for reading programs that respect these cultural and linguistic differences and the specifics of an existing reading program (BRIDGE), which seeks to move Black non-mainstreamed students' reading from African American Language to Standard English. The book sets forth the effectiveness of this program in large scale field tests, and the prospects for using this approach to break the cumulative deficit cycle among Black non-mainstream students.

2

The Deficit and Difference Models

Since the late fifties, there has been a plethora of research by psychologists and educators on the subject of the education of Black children. The impetus for this research was the massive pattern of academic failure displayed by Black children in this country's public schools as documented by standardized test scores.

With an abundance of government and private foundation monies available, numerous researchers in academia became experts on Black inner-city children and their families. It is important to note that social science research tends to design and then follow the money trail.

At that time in history one of the best ways to obtain a research grant was to show interest in the educational problems of inner-city residents. The environment of the Black community, in general, and the culture of Blacks, in particular, became the concern of a new generation of researchers.

An impressive amount of literature was generated on the study of the so-called 'disadvantaged.' The 'deficit model', sometimes referred to as the 'social pathology model', or the 'deficiency hypothesis' became the 'model of choice' for social scientists. This model asserts that Black children are deficient in cognitive, linguistic and general intellectual skills and in their development. According to the deficit model, Black people, when compared to White people, were deficit in a measurable trait (construct) called intelligence.

In the nineteenth century all attempts to measure physical characteristics of race as a basis for differences in ability and intelligence ended in failure (Prichard, 1851; Stanton, 1960). Theories of innate inferiority, though plentiful in number, had no substantial evidence to support them. When the intelligence test was introduced by Alfred Binet and Theodore Simon, it scarcely mattered how the races differed physically; now a scientific instrument had been developed which seemed to validate the intellectual inferiority of all non-white races.

Terman (1916) the father of American intelligence testing, observed that his intelligence test showed that low intelligence was a common trait among Negroes.

> ...it (low intelligence) is very, very common...among Negroes. Their dullness seems to be racial, or at least inherent in the family stock from which they come...The whole question of racial difference in mental traits will have to be taken up anew by experimental methods...The writer predicts that when this is done there will be discovered enormously significant racial differences in general intelligence, differences which cannot be wiped out by any scheme of mental culture...(such experiments will prove that many Black children are)...uneducatable beyond the merest rudiments of training. No amount of school instruction will ever make them intelligent voters, or capable citizens in the true sense of the word (Terman).

Since 1916, a great deal of experimental research has been conducted on Blacks using intelligence tests. Kennedy, Vernon and White (1963) indicated that the "cumulative effects of deprivation, the trend toward low IQ's among Black children, intensifies over time. They reported a significant negative correlation between age and IQ in their sample of 1,800 Black school children. They found that the mean IQ for Black elementary school children in their sample was 86 at the age of five and 65 at the age of thirteen. Osborn (1960) obtained similar results in a longitudinal study of racial differences and school achievement.

Deutsch and Brown (1964) examined the scores of 543 urban school children on the Lorge-Thorndike Intelligence Test stratified by race, social class, and grade level. They found Black children scored lower than White children regardless of social class. When Black and White children are compared on intelligence tests, generally, Blacks score lower on measured intelligence than Whites. Similar findings have been reported by Garrett (1961), Humphreys (1969) and Shuey (1958).

Arthur Jensen (1969), after extensively reviewing the scientific literature and research on intelligence and race in this country, reported that Blacks score, on the average, one standard deviation or approximately 15 IQ points lower than Whites. Jensen (1973) points out that a "deficit" of one standard deviation in IQ cannot be taken lightly or considered to be inconsequential.

> A difference of one standard deviation can hardly be called inconsequential. Intelligence tests have more than proven themselves as a valid predictor...Unpleasant as these predictions may seem to some people, their significance cannot be wished away because of beliefs in equality...An average difference of one standard deviation between Blacks and Whites means that the White population will have seven times the percentage

of potentially gifted talented persons (i.e. IQ's over 115) as the Black population...that mental retardation will occur seven times as often among Blacks as among Whites.

Hernstein and Murray, epitomize contemporary deficit theorists in their book, The Bell Curve (1994). They lead the reader to conclude that affirmative action and educational intervention programs are a waste of resources that should be diverted to the gifted. They put forth the view, or better stated assumption, that intelligence is a single, immutable trait. They would have their readers believe that a simple 'paper and pencil' test taps the core of intelligence; 'g' (general intelligence). For Hernstein and Murray, inequality in America for Blacks is explained by low IQ scores, or low 'g'. And following this line of reasoning, work on social conditioning and educational intervention cannot be effective.

In many ways Hernstein and Murray and Terman, have identical views. Terman believed that no amount of school or instruction would ever make Black children "intelligent voters or capable citizens" due to their low general intelligence. The two, Hernstein and Murray and Terman, present deficit model views from a historical and contemporary vantage point.

Language

The language Black children bring to school has been identified in the literature as one of the major causal factors contributing to deficits in learning and cognition. Beginning in the sixties, the language or dialect of Blacks became a major topic of research interest. Jones (1960), after examining differential scoring on intelligence tests, concluded Blacks' "lack of facility in the use of English language...was astounding." Jones assumed that this deficiency was caused by the 'common use of dialects by southern Negroes.' She concluded that these dialects are "substantially oral shorthand" and "an underdeveloped language which may restrict the average Negroes' perceptual discrimination and concept formation."

A similar position was taken by Engelman (1967). He stated, "too frequently, a four year old child of poverty does not understand the meaning of such words as long, full, animal, red....Too frequently he cannot repeat a simple statement such as 'the bread is under the oven' even after he has been given four trials."

Bereiter and Engelman (1966) reported that the language of disadvantaged children consists of gestures, single words and a series of poorly connected words and phrases. They speculated that verbal deprivation is the primary reason for the failure of Black children in the public schools. Bereiter and Engelman stated, "the disadvantaged child has not learned the rules that are necessary for defining concepts, for drawing inferences, for asking questions and for giving explanations."

Environment and Culture

The environment of the Black community, in general, and the culture of Blacks, in particular, has been the concern of many researchers. The notion of "cultural deprivation" has been advanced and accepted by numerous researchers (Bloom, 1965; Deutsch, et al., 1967; Glazer and Moynihan, 1963; Hunt, 1961).

Proponents of the cultural deprivation hypotheses argue that the culture and environment and family structure of the Black community retard cognitive and linguistic growth (Bereiter, 1965; Hurst. 1965; Johnson, 1970). According to Deutsch (1963), speech patterns of the lower class homes may be a causal factor leading to deficits in the children's language development.

In observations of lower class homes, it appears that
speech sequences seem to be temporally very limited
and poorly constructed syntactically. It is thus not sur-
prising to find that a major focus of deficit in the
children's language development is syntactical organization and subject continuity.

Green (1964) stated, it is not only the "inadequate" speech
used in the Black disadvantaged home environment that contrib-
utes to language deficits, but also the speech used outside of school
in the children's peer group and community.

The very inadequate speech that is used in the home
is also used in the neighborhood, on the playground
and in the classroom. Since these poor English patterns are reconstructed constantly by the associations
that these young people have, the school has to play a
strong role in bringing about a change...

Hunt (1961) concluded that the environment of the Black
community and more specifically, the Black inner-city mother,
do not provide Black children with adequate social and sensory
stimulation. A similar position was taken by Martin Deutsch
(1963). Deutsch reported that Black inner-city children experienced a form of stimulus deprivation which leads to cognitive
and linguistic deficits. He hypothesized that stimulus deprivation
is caused by a lack of toys, books and adequate models of language usage in the Black home and surrounding community.

Cynthia Deutsch (1964) put forth a contrary thesis. She es-
poused the view that sensory stimulation in the Black home is
excessive. She asserts that the high noise level in the Black home,
coupled with simultaneous inputs: TV, record players, and conversations often happening at the same time), cause the children to
tune out all stimulation, thus creating a vacuum for themselves.

McClelland (1968) attributes a lack of achievement motivation among Black children to failure in the socialization process of the Black home. He hypothesized that the socialization failure of Black children is caused by the matricentric structure of the Black family and the persistence of child-rearing practices which originated during slavery.

Hess, Shipman, Brophy and Bear (1968) concluded that maternal language style is a major contributing factor of Black children's language deficits. They held that the differences (when compared to middle class mothers) in maternal language and teaching styles cause disadvantaged children to be almost uneducable.

Assumptions of the Deficit Model

In the mid-sixties, the War on Poverty was declared. Spurred by urban violence and unrest, the assassination of a popular president and the Civil Rights act of 1964, America undertook a massive effort to address long-standing and sorely neglected problems of poverty and mounting frustration among the nation's poor. The major focus of this effort was pushed by the Black population who were no longer content to be invisible, to accept docilely their station in American society. The education of Black "disadvantaged" children was selected as a primary target for the war.

Gunnings (1972) describes the emergence of the War on Poverty:

> Early in 1964, the nation was awakened to the inadequacy of existing education for poor, disadvantaged, economically deprived children. Black Americans, particularly, had aroused the nation's conscience to the deprivation and injustices they were suffering. Partly as a conciliatory effort to appease a group that would not let the nation relax, as a therapeutic process to relieve

the nation's guilty conscience, and as a commemora-
tive gesture to a slain president, the War on Poverty
was instituted. The immediate result was the enactment
of legislation...which provided for the establishment
of...community action programs. These programs were
aimed at the children who were going to be or had
been losers in the regular school program. The purpose
of these programs, compensatory in nature, was established as the improvement of the social, psychological, economical and educational welfare of the participants.

Sponsored by the federal government and strongly supported
by private foundations, a great many intervention programs were
instituted. The major target of these programs were the disadvantaged. The term "disadvantaged" became a euphemism for non-
mainstream Blacks and other minorities. The educational area was
chosen as the major battlefield.

The Anti-Poverty Program, the popular name for the War on
Poverty, was launched with a great deal of enthusiasm, idealism,
high expectations and fanfare. Its educational intervention programs were firmly based on what was considered to be a comprehensive body of research documenting the cause of the educational deficits of Black children.

Unfortunately, the War on Poverty, for many reasons, never
lived up to initial expectations. Confronted with controversy, failure and criticism, the Anti-Poverty Program slowly ebbed out of
existence. Goldenberg (1973) wrote concerning the demise of the
War on Poverty:

In hindsight, let us be clear about the fact that the late,
lamented War on Poverty, especially in terms of the

social theory upon which it was based...was never really intended to be a war at all... Unlike the "target population" for whom it was intended, the War on Poverty was created by people whose faith in America and its institutions was as unshaken as their belief that poverty could be eliminated (and quickly, we might add) through the development of a massive program of individual remediation...

Although the reasons for the failure of the Anti-Poverty Program to live up to expectations are numerous (bureaucratic conservatism, mismanagement, widely publicized failure of some of its programs, questionable evaluation practices, etc.), many researchers agree that the primary cause was in the area of program assumptions. The Anti-Poverty Program's intervention programs were a direct product of social science research based on the deficit model. They relied on the deficit model research for their scientific validity and programmatic direction. A set of interlocking assumptions concerning the "disadvantaged" became the super-structure of these intervention programs. These assumptions were, at the time, believed to be "scientific facts," documented by mountains of "hard data."

Stephen and Joan Baratz (1970) examined the underlying assumptions of intervention programs associated with the War on Poverty. They suggested that the failure of social research to recognize existing cultural forms of the Black community doomed intervention programs, such as Head Start, to failure before they ever got off the drafting board. They stated:

It is important to understand that the entire intervention model of Head Start rests on the assumption of linguistic and cognitive deficits which must be remediated if the child is to succeed in school.

The Baratzes suggested that the ethnocentric view of the social scientists toward the Black community provided educators with
a distorted image of the life patterns of that community. This distorted image, according to the Baratzes, was translated into the rationale of social action programs. The objectives of those programs
was to improve the children's language and cognitive skills by alter-
ing the culture, home environment, and child rearing practices of
the Black family. They stated that most intervention programs of
the sixties failed because their goal was to correct deficits in Black
children that simply did not exist, rather than to intervene in the
school systems and mainstream institutions that create the problems.

One can postulate that the educational problems of Black non-
mainstream children are heightened by the assumptions on which
intervention programs are based. These assumptions lead inter-
ventionists to view the educational problems as Black problems
rather than problem of institutional failure.

The problem is perceived, first and foremost, as a Black problem. The children, Black non-mainstream children, do not fit the
mainstream institutions and way of life. They are often mismatched
along the variables of language, culture and life styles. Following a
simplistic and often syllogistic line of reasoning, it is concluded
that there is something 'wrong with" or "deficient in" Black non-
mainstream children. This alleged deficiency calls for intervention
and massive remediation in order to get the children to match the
mainstream institutions and way of life.

These interlocking assumptions, or mis-assumptions, which
were considered to be well grounded in research, lead interven-
tionists to:

1. Employ such concepts as the "middle class measuring rod,"
    "Core Culture," and "culturally deprived" in the formula-
    tion and design of intervention programs.

2. Use standard American English, the language spoken by the middle and upper classes, as a measure of linguistic competency and cognitive capacity and to conceptualize the language spoken by Black children, African American Language, as a deficient form of standard American English rather than a different dialect.

3. Conceptualize Black cultural conventions, especially the organization of the Black home and child rearing practices, that is, mother-child patterns, as the product of a defective culture which produces linguistically and cognitively impaired children who cannot learn.

4. Attempt to intervene, at the earliest possible period, in the cultural environment of Black children under the rubric of enrichment—the infusion of White middle class cultural values, aspirations, beliefs and experiences-to compensate for alleged deficiencies.

The overall failure of intervention programs based on the deficit model to improve the educational plight of "disadvantaged" children was due, in large part, to educators' and social scientists' inability to separate scientific fact from cultural ethnocentrism. Educators and social scientists, as a product of their culture, saw only what their culture taught them to see. They carried their cultural ethnocentrism into their science and used it as a basis for evaluating the academic failure of Black children.

The Cultural Differences Model

In contrast to the deficit model, an alternative view of the educational problems of Black children in the public schools is the cultural difference model. The cultural difference model postulates that the Black Child's language, culture, family structure and life style are not deficient, but different from those of their middle class counterparts. It is in direct opposition to the deficit model. The cultural difference model takes the position that difference observed in intelligence testing, cultural conventions and the language used in the Black community are not the results of faulty learning, pathology or genetic inferiority. These differences represent the manifestations of a unique African American culture.

It is acknowledged by the difference model that Black Americans and White Americans come from observably different cultural backgrounds. These different backgrounds emphasize different learning experiences, values and 'ways of doing things' that are viewed as necessary for survival.

According to this model, observations that Black Americans are different from White Americans should not be interpreted as evidence of inferiority, defensiveness or pathology. The cultural difference model allows ethnic populations to be unique and different without the assumption of inferiority. It makes a distinction between equality and uniformity. It asserts that American educators and social scientists have confused equality with uniformity.

Stephen and Joan Baratz, in their critique of social science research on African Americans observed that research conducted on Black groups was based on an "idealized norm of American behavior" against which all behavior is measured." This norm is defined by, and defines the way White middle class America is supposed to behave.

Researchers accepted the egalitarian principle; all men are equal under the law and should be treated as such. These researchers, "however wrongly, equated equality with sameness." In attempting to apply this misinterpretation of egalitarian principle, social scientists were left with the dubious task of describing Black behavior "not as it is, but rather as it deviates from the normative system defined by the White middle class."

Cronbach noted that intelligent behavior involves a cultural judgment:

> We must accept Liverant's...conclusion that to decide "what is or is not intelligent behavior involves a cultural judgment" and that a person's variation in efficiency from task to task must be explained by examining his expectations and the rewards available.

A growing number of researchers have begun to point out the limitations and cultural bias of tests used for the assessment of Black children. Most of the tests used by the schools discriminate against speakers of African American Language because the items used on the tests are middle class specific and presented in language not familiar to most speakers of African American Language. William and Rivers (1975) state:

> It is general knowledge that the major standardized tests place exceedingly strong emphasis on verbal skills. In fact, the very popular WISC and Binet may be considered tests of conventional verbal skills.

There are certain inherent problems in testing Black culturally different children:

a) standardized tests in their present composition are biased in favor of those children whose primary language is standard English and whose culture and value system is that of mainstream White middle class America;

b) educational programs are biased against those children whose primary language is African American Language and whose culture and value system is that of Black, non-mainstream culture;

c) the structural similarity and content of items in educational
    programs and in ability tests are nearly identical.

Given the relationship between the standardized tests and
the measures of school performance and the educational programs
in the schools, one would expect a high correlation between standardized test scores and school performance. Black culturally different children who score low on the tests also tend to do poorly
in school because both the tests and the schools are biased against
their language and culture, and both are almost identical in structure and content of items.

Language Differences

Beginning in the latter half of the sixties, a body of scientific literature appeared which considers the language of Black so-called
"disadvantaged" children as a *different* rather than a deficient
form of English (Baratz, 1968; Cazden, 1966; Labov and Cohen,
1967; Steward, 1967, 1968).

With growing recognition in the literature of the existence
of a different language system spoken by many Blacks in this
country, a series of studies were conducted to describe and ana-
lyze the features of that language system. Bailey (1965, 1968),
Dillard (1967), Labov (1967) and Steward (1967, 1968) reported
that differences between standardized English and the language
spoken by many Blacks (sometimes referred to as Black English, Black Vernacular, Black non-standard English, or Black
dialect) occur in varying degrees in regard to the sound system,
vocabulary and grammar.

Additional evidence in support of the language difference position as opposed to the language deficiency position was derived
from the words of Cazden, Labov and Moore (1968, 1971). Moore
and Labov found that 'disadvantaged" Black children developed

syntactic rules (plurals, negation, past markers, possessives, etc.) to the same degree as middle class children. Cazden (1967) found that the syntactic rules of lower class Black children and middle class children develop at the same pace. Moore (1971) concluded that Black children do not have rules missing from their grammar and do not lag behind middle class children in the acquisition of the rules in the early periods of grammar development.

In response to the language deficit position that Black children from inner-city areas receive little verbal stimulation, hear very little well formed language, cannot speak complete sentences, do not know the names of common objects, and cannot form concepts or convey logical thought, Labov (1969) stated:

> Unfortunately, these notions of language deficits are based on the works of educational psychologists who know very little about language and even less about Negro children. The concept of verbal deprivation has no basis in social reality: In fact Negro children from the ghetto area receive a great deal of verbal stimulation, hear more well-formed sentences than middle-class children, and participate fully in a highly developed verbal culture; they have the same basic vocabulary, possess the same capacity for conceptual learning and use the same logic as anyone else who learns to speak and understand English.
>
> The notion of verbal deprecation is part of the modern mythology of educational psychology, typical of the unfounded notions which tend to spread rapidly in our educational system.

Baratz (1969) questioned Cynthia Deutsch's (1964) findings on the deficient auditory discrimination of Black "disadvantaged" children when compared to White middle class children.

It is no wonder then, that Cynthia Deutsch should find from her assessment of auditory discrimination that disadvantaged Black children do not "discriminate" as well as White children from middle class linguistic environments. She administered a discrimination task that equated "correct responses" with judgments or equivalences and differences in standard English sound usage. Many of her stimuli, (e.g., pin-pen), are similar for the Negro non-standard speaker. She attributed the difference in performance of disadvantaged children to such things as the constant glare of the television in their homes, and there being so much "noise" in their environment that the children tended to "time out." However, Black children make responses based on the kind of language they consider appropriate…In the same way that cot (for sleeping) and caught (for ensnared); or marry (to wed), Mary (the girl), and merry (to be happy) are not distinguished in the speech of many White people…pin and pen are the same in the language of many ghetto Blacks (Baratz, 1968).

Baratz, in the same article, reports the results of a sentence repetition task study. The study was similar to the one performed by Engelmann (1967) from which he concluded that Black children cannot repeat a simple statement. Baratz, unlike Engelmann however, used sentences in standard English and in non-standard English. Examples of the two sets of sentences are:

Standard English

"I asked Tom if he wanted to go to the picture that was playing at the Howard."

Non-Standard English

"I asks Tom do he wanta go to the picture that be playin' the Howard."

The results of the study were as follows:

> As expected, the results of the sentence-repetition indicated that Whites were superior to Negroes in repeating standard English sentences, but on the other hand, Negroes were far superior to Whites in repeating Negro non-standard English sentences. Performance of the various sentences was influenced far more by the race of the child than by his age.

Baratz concluded from her study:

> The fact that standard and non-standard speakers exhibited similar translation behaviors when confronted with sentences that were outside of the primary code indicates quite clearly that the language deficiency that has so often been attributed to the low income Negro is not a language deficit so much as a difficulty in code switching when the second code (standard English) is not as well learned as the first (non-standard English) (Baratz, 1968).

To explain why Black children receive lower scores on psychological tests of cognitive abilities and on tests given in the schools, Williams and Rivers (1975) conducted a study similar to the one conducted by Baratz. They translated the Boehm Test of Basic Concepts into two versions: a standard version and a non-standard version. The Boehm Test was administered under two conditions, the standard version of the test instructions and the non-standard version of test instructions, to 990 Black, elementary children in the St. Louis public school system. The results of their experiment indicated that the mean score of the non-standard group on the non-standard version was significantly higher than that of the standard group on the standard version. Williams and Rivers concluded that:

> The results...certainly indicate that Black children are penalized by instructions on group tests which are presented in standard English. However, the results also indicate that when the language in test instructions is modified to be more compatible with the dialectic environment in which the child is familiar, he performs as well as, and in some cases, better than high socio-economic children...

Williams and Rivers attributed the academic failure of Black children to a "mismatch" between the language and culture of the children and the language and culture of the tests and educational programs employed by the public schools.

Black, non-mainstream children possess the same cognitive apparatus and abilities as mainstream children. Differences in academic performance occur because the cognitive apparatus of these children is often differently triggered by the cultural context of the language used. The different triggering of the students' cognitive apparatus often causes learning to be more effective for Black, non-mainstream students "in the streets" than in the classroom; and that the students must perform an added cognitive operation in order to grasp many of the concepts taught in the schools. The students must translate incoming conceptual material into a familiar cultural context in order to assimilate it.

Assumptions and Discussion of the Cultural Difference Model

Beginning in the mid-sixties, coinciding with the launch of the War on Poverty, the cultural differences position, a counter-argument to the deficit position, started appearing in the language literature. The cultural difference theorists based their argument on the then recent discovery by linguists that Black, urban inner-city dwellers possess a consistent, though different, rule-governed linguistic system. They called for a revolution in scientific thought concerning Black people. They challenged the deficit assumptions, which relied heavily on data from language research and standardized tests, on the basis that deviations from the mainstream normative patterns were falsely interpreted as deficits. Stephen and Joan Baratz (1970) state:

> The major support for the assertion of revolution in scientific thinking about the Negro comes from the discovery that the urban Negro has a consistent, though different, linguistic system. This discovery is an anomaly in that it could not have been predicted from the social pathology paradigm. This finding...violates many of the perceptions and expectations about Negro behavior which are built into the assumptive base of the social pathology model. This assumptive base, it is argued, has restricted our phenomenological field to deviations from normative behavior rather than to descriptions of different normative configurations.

Both the proponents of the deficit position and the cultural difference position agree that Black children are failing in the school and that something should be done. They differ on the cause of the failure and the course of intervention. Proponents of the cultural difference position reflect deficit model assumptions that the cause is the children's apparent unreadiness for school, and that intervention programs should be focused on the children's language, family and socio-cultural system in order to bring them in line with the schools and the mainstream society. Cultural difference proponents argue that America is a poly-cultural society with a mono-cultural school system. They make the assumption that the school's unwillingness to accommodate to the children's language and culture is the cause, and that intervention should be focused at the level of the schools, its teachers, and curricula rather than at the level of the children.

Unlike the deficit model, very few government and foundation sponsored intervention programs have emerged from the cultural difference model. Although there is an increasing amount of theoretical literature on the cultural difference position, very little applied research and development has taken place. At the present time, this is to be expected, owing to the relative newness of the model and the poverty of government and foundation funds for basic research and development. An extensive search of the literature failed to reveal sizable government or foundation sponsored intervention programs.

Although there is a great deal of diversity within the cultural difference position, some of the assumptions upon which intervention programs could and undoubtedly will be based in the future, can be stated with a high degree of agreement among proponents of the position:

1. No language or dialect is structurally superior to another language or dialect (DeStefano, 1973).
2. Every language variety is systematic and ordered. African American Language is not irregular or haphazard and is not an aberration of a more standard form of English (Wolfram, 1970; Labov, 1969).

3. Language and culture are inextricably bound together. To deny one's language or dialect is to deny one's culture; to disparage a person's language is to disparage a person's culture (Goodman, 1965; Simpkins, Gunnings, and Keatney, 1972).

4. A person cannot be cognitively less competent than is necessary to master the vastly complex rule system of his/her native language (Cole, Gay, Glick, and Sharp, 1971; Simpkins, 1976).

5. Differences in performance on standardized tests of cognitive abilities reside more in the situation and cultural context to which particular cognitive processes are applied than in the existence of a cognitive process or structure is on cultural or racial group and its absence in others (Cole, Gay, Glick, and Sharp, 1971; Labov, 1969; Simpkins, 1976; Williams, 1975).

The cultural difference model and its concomitant assumptions appear to hold the promise that intervention programs will be designed to take into consideration the language and culture of Black children and draw on their strengths rather than their weaknesses. However, one must anticipate that there will be some resistance to adopting the cultural difference position. Stephen and Joan Baratz (1970) state:

> ...there may be resistance to adopting the cultural difference model which stems not only from the inherent methodologies of the social pathology theory, but also from the...often unexpressed socio-political view of our current racial situation — views which are unarticulated and therefore unexamined. Thus, the resistance we anticipate may be intensified by the fear that talking about differences in Negro behavior may automatically produce in the social pathologist the postulation of genetic differences.

At the present time, there are few concrete extensions of the cultural differences model in this country's school system. Thus the effectiveness of this position cannot be demonstrated due to the lack of programs which are based on this model or a contrast in effects with the deficit position.

This lack of programmatic extensions of the culturally different model is due primarily to a lack of government and private foundations funding. While an abundance of funding has been available for deficit model research, the funds dried up when linguists and other researchers began to point out through their research activities that the language spoken by Black non-mainstream children and their families was rule governed, systematic and in no way inferior to, or a distorted version of standard English. This, coupled with their insistence that schools should respect the language and culture that the children bring to the schools and use it as a platform to build standard language skills, appears to have had a profound effect on the funding situation.

3

Cultural Ethnocentrism

The Relationship of Public Education and Social Science Research to the "Failure" of Black Non-Mainstream Students

"Whites can give lip service to Afro-American culture as legitimate and creative, to the Black man as psychologically and culturally adequate, as long as they can be assured that he is really more White than anything else. As long as Whites can conceive of him as being a 'Black-White man,' he will be psychologically and culturally more palatable to them.

It places the Black man in this country in a perpetual position of inferiority. For the Black man becomes a 'Sick White man' who never quite measures up to the real White man, who in turn becomes the standard of measurement."

(Simpkins, Williams and Gunning, 1971)

Historically, the socialization of poor and ethnic group students has been one of the primary and overriding objectives of

American education. The major goal of the public schools, when they were first established in the late 1800's was to create students who were similar in aspirations, attitudes, values, language usage and cultural trappings. Central to this goal was belief in the concept of the "melting pot," which asserted that diverse ethnic groups would be blended to produce one nationality with English as a common language, Western Europe as a culture and the middle and upper classes as models of excellence. According to the melting pot concept, these groups would shed their ethnic impurities and blend into the great American mainstream.

The common school in America was based on the premise that "all men are created equal," and therefore, there should be equal treatment for all.

> "On the surface "equal treatment for all" seemed laudable as a purpose. When bureaucratic organizations tried to act upon it, however, they found it administratively convenient to achieve equal treatment by treating everyone as if they were alike." (Erickson and Krumbein, 1971)

American educators, following in the tradition of Dewey, attempted, with the zeal of missionaries, "to see to it that each individual [got] an opportunity to escape from the limitations of the social group in which he was born."

No doubt Dewey meant well when he spoke in liberal opinion of "liberating the individual from the limitations of the social group to which he belongs." But there is an inherently patronizing quality in the concept "limitation." Limitation may mean poverty; it is clear that to Dewey it also meant cultural difference. (Erickson and Krumbein, 1971).

American educators assumed a two-fold role with respect to Black students—that of socializer and that of oppressor. As socializers, it was their appointed task, as they viewed it, to impose a single standard of behavior: the Americanization of Black students. Following an industrial model, they attempted to take in raw materials (Black students) and turn out a finished product according to specifications. It was their goal to produce a finished product in the areas of verbal behavior, aspiration, attitude and values. As oppressors, it was their chosen task to eradicate what they believed to be a defective and inferior "subculture." They considered Black culture to be a subculture—a grotesque distortion of American culture resulting from the conditions of slavery and its aftermath, the urban ghetto, and rural poverty. It was their belief that this defective subculture prevented Black students from being properly educated and assimilated into the great American mainstream.

American educators spotlighted those Blacks who "had made it" via the schools—those Blacks who had become "Educated" and achieved upward mobility in the American mainstream. They proudly held up their success to Black America. They vocally informed Black students that they could become just like the success models if they applied themselves, worked hard and "got a good education." Black students could not help but notice that the Black doctors, lawyers, educators, scientists and other success models were culturally more White than anything else, they were "Black-White men." The message to Black students was clear: If you want to become educated and achieve "the good life," you must become similar to White mainstream people. Many Black students have looked at the success models held up for them to emulate and said to themselves, "Yeah, they made it. But besides they skin, them ain't nothing like me. And I don't think I can or wanta be anything like them."

Cultural Accommodation

Black social scientists and educators have for a long time recognized that in order to be successful in the American education system, Black students must assimilate mainstream American culture. The closer Black students are to the mainstream culture in their language, interests, learning and life styles, the higher the probability for successful achievement in the schools.

> "The public school system has become the major sorting mechanism in this society and the major means of instilling social control. In doing so it seems to have become, as well, the major agency involved in the creation and evolution of model middle class values...
>
> In addition, there is a cluster of sociocultural traits involved that are necessary for success in the schools, which contain such obvious matters as language, including dialect and accent; religion and dress and more subtle values and attitudes. Again, the classification is in terms of a presumed Anglo-Saxon, Puritan ideal of questionable historicity; inner directed, individually responsible, morally upright, rationally and emotionally restrained, ambitious but socially unostentatious, competitive, prudent of time, money and self (Dickman, 1973)."

The further removed Black students are from the mainstream culture, or better stated, the closer they are to Black non-mainstream culture in their language, interests, values, learning and life styles, the lower the probability for their successful achievement in the schools.

> "The schools, as representatives of the larger society, virtually ignore the values of these groups, while embracing the perspective of the 'White Anglo-Saxon

Ideal.' Thus, there appears to be a direct relationship between the degree to which a group's values, norms and standards are excluded from the dominant values of the society and the failure of the society's schools to educate its members. Apparently, the schools, as subsystems of the larger societal system, reflect the dominant trends of the society, vis-a-vis its powerless minorities (Barnes, 1974)."

This is not a new phenomenon or observation. In fact, it is as old as slavery and as American as racism.

Black mothers, historically, have been forced to host the oppressors. Black mothers have been forced to teach their children to accommodate to White mainstream culture in order for their children to survive. Many Black children have heard their mothers say, "I'll kill you myself before I let them kill you. You gonna have to learn." This behavior has its roots in the American system of slavery. It was once, for Black people, a functional coping mechanism against the harsh, oppressive, dehumanizing effects of slavery. Across time, this cultural accommodation on the part of Blacks to White culture became accepted by both Black and White educators as the best, and possibly the only way for Blacks to become "educated."

If Black people are educated, they are expected to display the refinement of White culture–especially in their verbal behavior. It was, and it is today, for White people and unfortunately for a great many Black professionals, a massive, mind-boggling paradox for a Black man to be intelligent and "educated" and to cling to Black non-mainstream culture. Cobbs and Grier, two Black psychiatrists, related in their book *Black Rage*, the case of a Black man who was a doctoral candidate in speech, but clung tenaciously to his African American Language; or as Cobbs and Grier put it, "his outrageous pathos." Cobbs and Grier explained this contradiction in the classical Freudian mode: The man's bizarre verbal behavior was pathological, resulting from early childhood interactions with his mother, with definite sexual implications.

If Black people did not assimilate White mainstream culture, their "education," as well as their intelligence, was suspect; and in some cases their sanity—all of which have a direct bearing on determining whether or not they would succeed in acquiring "the good life."

> "To succeed...the individual must abandon most of the cultural traits of his home, except for those few, stripped of all real symbolic significance, which the dominant society deems tolerable. Those behaviors, values and attitudes which he must abandon are those emotionally embedded, acquired as they were in the context of infancy and early childhood. To do so he must disrupt his ties to his group of origin. What is demanded, then, is a rejection of his affiliation with kin and community, of his ties to his group of birth. What this means is a rejection of those emotional bonds with family and community (Dickeman, 1973)."

Problems with Cultural Accommodation

Though both Black and White educators seem to agree that in order to become educated and thus have access to the good life, Black students must take the route of mainstream culture, there were, nevertheless, some major problems with this approach. Visible numbers of Black students were refusing to become enculturated into mainstream culture. This occurred particularly in the area of verbal behavior. Despite massive efforts on the part

of the schools, Black students still clung tenaciously to their dialect and culture.

In addition, educators and social scientists began to observe
that these same students were not substantially benefitting from
this country's educational system. They asked why. The answers
most frequently heard were based on biological explanation to
account for racial differences—and genetic inferiority. By the
sixties, educators and social scientists began to seriously chal-
lenge biological explanations and turn toward environmental social class explanations.

> "Gradually, however, with an occasional throwback
> or backlash, educators and scientists by the sixties be-
> gan seriously to challenge the absurdity of biological
> explanations and to shift to the other equally absurd
> social class explanations (Erickson, Bryan and Walker,
> 1972)."

The failure of Black non-mainstream children in the American public school system was explained on the basis of the
children's being "culturally deprived" when they entered school.
This view held that Black non-mainstream children brought to
school a language, culture and motivational system that was not
conducive to educational achievement. The cultural environment
of the Black community retarded the children's cognitive and linguistic growth. The solution most often recommended was enrichment (a healthy shot of good White mainstream culture).

> "One approach particularly in vogue in the early
> sixties...was the theme that many children are "cultur-
> ally deprived" when they enter school. From the
> "culturally deprived" view, White middle class children
> are assured to have the benefit of exposure to a more

enriched culture than lower class (particularly non-
white) children (Erickson, Bryan and Walker, 1972)."

Social scientists, equipped with the American missionary men-
tality and a mainstream measuring rod began descending upon
unsuspecting Black communities throughout the country in order to help them solve their educational problems through the
miracle of modern research activities.

> "There is very little in the research literature that is
> complimentary to the Black child. Generally, he is por-
> trayed as a scholastically deprived drag on the educa-
> tional system of this country...
>
> However, there has been no scarcity of sociologi-
> cal, psychological and educational missionaries wait-
> ing to rescue him from the depths of intellectual and
> social obscurity...The amount of money spent re-
> searching Black children over the years attests to the
> favor of these scientists. However, it is unfortunate
> that their efforts have been directed toward "victim
> analysis" rather than toward ways in which the basic
> positive, natural abilities of these children may be as-
> sessed and used in the development of valid educa-
> tional systems (Rivers, 1973)."

These social scientists, in their misguided efforts to rescue
Black non-mainstream children, studded the scientific literature
with damaging labels and concepts to explain the Black child's
"condition."

Over the years White experts have generated euphemistic
labels for Black children such as "culturally deprived," "culturally disadvantaged," and "culturally deficient." Each label

implicitly and explicitly points to an alleged deficiency, weakness, or absence of a quality in the Black American (Simpkins, Williams and Cummings, 1971).

Black protest groups in the form of "Black caucuses" started appearing on the social science scene in the mid-sixties. When Black social scientists began to point out that these labels and the concepts that they conveyed were of a pejorative nature, embodying myths, stereotypes, faulty and often racist assumptions about Black people, they were accused of being oversensitive and preoccupied with semantic irrelevancies. Their White counterparts began to state that they did not know what to call Black people because Blacks got offended by any and all labels they used. They stated that such nitpicking diverted attention from the real and pressing problems of Blacks. Some went on to state that perhaps the real problem was not in the labels used, but that Blacks were offended by Whites pointing out their obvious shortcomings; that Blacks do not understand that the prerequisite for intervention and eventual solution is honest recognition of the problem.

While working on an instructional reading program for Black non-mainstream students at a publishing company, a paper came across my desk. The paper was titled, "The Culturally Deprived Reader: Research, Diagnosis and Prescriptions." The following comments were written on the front page of the paper: "A good review—outlines problems and their causes..." The phrase "culturally deprived reader" immediately caught my attention. The title brought to mind children who have spent their lives locked in a closet, or who have been raised by animals, or have experienced some other form of isolation from humans, and thus were culturally deprived. On the first page, the author of the paper presented her rationale for using the term "culturally deprived."

"In this report, 'culturally deprived' and similar terms
are utilized for cataloging efficiency, with the understanding that the "deprived" culture is still rich in
tradition...It is deprived, then, not of culture in the
anthropological sense, but perhaps of some standardized middle class culture."

The author went on to state what, for Blacks, has become a
very familiar rationalization employed by social scientists:

"Only by identifying the child as he is can we take
him from where he is to where he ought to be so that
he may live a life of self-fulfillment and creativity. With
this qualification, it is hoped that referential phrases
may be taken as objective rather than as objection-
ably contemptuous terms (Serage, 1973)."

Several questions immediately come to mind upon reading
the author's rationale for the choice of terms: (1) How does em-
ploying illogical, unscientific (in an anthropological sense), and
probably racist labels lead to cataloging efficiency? (2) How can
such labels be taken as objective when they so grossly violate the
most basic definition of objectivity as used in science?

The author approached the problem of academic failure of
Black non-mainstream children in the public schools from a typical mainstream perspective. Her approach, unfortunately, is representative of a great many educators and social scientists. The
problem is perceived, first and foremost, as a Black problem. The
children do not fit the mainstream institutions and way of life.
*They are often mismatched along with variables of language,
culture, learning and life styles.* Following a simplistic and often
syllogistic line of reasoning, it is concluded that there is something "wrong with" or "deficient in" Black non-mainstream

children. This alleged deficiency calls for intervention and massive remediation in order to get the children to match the mainstream institutions and way of life.

The Ugly American Syndrome

This faulty, ethnocentric reasoning appears to be based on the
following assumptions, which this author calls "The Ugly American Syndrome":

1. There is something intrinsically valuable about American
   mainstream culture and behavior which makes it the standard of comparison against which all other cultures and behaviors in this country can be evaluated.
2. To be different from American mainstream culture is a sign
   of deficiency, inferiority and/or pathology.
3. It is a misnomer to speak of Black non-mainstream culture.
   Or, to paraphrase Glazer and Moynihan: The Black man in
   this country is American and nothing else. The only culture he
   possesses is that of America. He has no unique values or culture to guide or protect himself (Glazer and Moynihan, 1963).

These assumptions and myths in the very recent past (in all
fairness it must be admitted that the situation is some what improved today, but not much) constitute a profound and axiomatic
belief—a general, shared position. This general position was never
questioned in itself. The position was held to be true because
there was consensus regarding it in the minds and hearts of mainstream educators and scientists. As a product of their culture,
they saw what their culture taught them to see. "What a man
sees depends both upon what he looks at, also what his previous
experience has taught him to see" (Kuhn, 1970).

Mainstream social scientists readily adopted the Ugly American Syndrome. They found it difficult to divorce themselves from their cultural ethnocentrism. They carried their cultural ethnocentrism into their science and used it as a basis for research on Black non-mainstream populations.

Conceptual Weakness of Research

The major weakness of research conducted on Black non-mainstream children was in the conceptual area. The investigators failed to realize the degree to which their cultural learning and value system influenced the questions they asked about Black non-mainstream children and the interpretations they gave to the data they collected to answer their questions. The primary reasons for this conceptual weakness seems to stem from the way social scientists view differences among people. The prevailing tendency was for social scientists to ignore, distort, and obliterate the role of cultural learning as an influence on behavior. Social scientists chose instead to embrace the myth of the "melting pot." They chose to believe that American society had become the melting pot where ethnic differences, in terms of a behavioral norm, have been transformed into a standardized, idealized norm of "American behavior."

They sought to explain, through their research activities, why Black non-mainstream children were behind White mainstream children in achievement scores. Rather than taking a critical look at mainstream culture and the products of that culture (schools and other institutions), they chose instead to search for deficits in the language, culture, motivational system and family structure of Black children, the victims of cultural ethnocentrism, cultural aggression, cultural accommodation and unequal educational, social and economic opportunities. Social scientists chose to find their answers in the symptoms, rather than to understand the condition.

Assumptive Explanations

The effects of these social scientists' mainstream cultural learning and value systems could be clearly seen in their invocation of purely assumptive explanations to explain why White mainstream children were successful in school and Black non-mainstream children were not. Assumptive explanations can be found throughout the research literature of the sixties and early seventies.

McClelland's (1969) Achievement Motivation Theory assumed a failure in the socialization process of the Black home. Blacks as a group are assumed to be lacking in the achievement motive (*n Ach*) because of the matricentric structure of the Black family and the persistence of child rearing practices that originated in slavery. "Negro slaves...developed child rearing practices calculated to produce obedience and responsibility, not *n Ach*. Their descendants, while free, should still show the effects of such training in loser *n Ach*, which is in fact exactly the case."

Katz (1967) assumed that achievement strivings are not socially recognized and reinforced by Black parents. He gives as an example helping with homework, which is at best an assumed mainstream route for success in school. Katz asserts that although Black parents verbalize high academic goals for their children, attainment is more difficult than verbalization, "especially when there are not models to imitate, and when achievement strivings are not socially recognized and reinforced by Negro parents."

Hunt (1968) assumed that the educational problems of Black non-mainstream children are caused by the failure of Black parents to provide adequate linguistic models. "These parents themselves often fail to utilize pre-positional relationships with precision and their syntax is confused. Thus, they serve as poor linguistic models for their young children."

Bereiter and Engelmann assumed verbal deprivation on the part of Black non-mainstream children to be the primary cause for the failure of Black children in the schools. Bereiter and Engelmann assert that Black children have a "primitive notion of the structure of language"; that the language of Black non-mainstream children "is not only merely an underdeveloped version of standard English, but is basically a non-logical mode of expressive behavior" composed primarily of gestures and "badly connected words and phrases." Bereiter and Engelmann assumed that, because of their lower class origin, the Black non-mainstream children "have not learned the language rules that are necessary for defining concepts; for drawing conclusions; for asking questions; and for giving explanations" (Berieter and Engelmann, 1968).

This type of research is worse than useless; it is extremely harmful. It supplies a "scientific" basis for the cultural ethnocentrism and institutional racism of America's public educational system. It serves to perpetuate the status quo—to maintain Black children in a position of educational inferiority. It transfers the blame for the educational system's failure to properly educate Black non-mainstream children squarely onto the shoulders of the Black community. It forces Black non-mainstream children to accommodate to the schools, rather than have the schools accommodate to the children; thus putting these children on a one-way street.

In the book *The Bell Curve: Intelligence and Class Structure in American Life* by Richard Hernstein and Charles Murray (1994), the argument is put forth that no amount of intervention in the schools or changes in public policy can take Black students, or for that matter African Americans in general, off this one way street. Reform of social science research (which this author believes is greatly needed) and reform of public schools' ethnic policies are simply an exercise in futility. According to Hernstein and Murray the problem is biological, low intelligence on the part of African Americans as measured by IQ tests. The authors of *The Bell Curve* assume that there is such a thing as 'g' (general intelligence) and lead their readers to conclude that African Americans possess lower amounts of 'g' and unfortunately, since it is biological or in the genes, very little, if anything can be done about it.

Reform of social science research is needed if social science research is to be used as a tool to promote "human welfare," rather than as an instrument for maintaining the status quo at the expense of oppressed peoples.

> "Black and White scholars involved in social research must challenge the centuries-old misuse of knowledge and power. New research, as well as the reinterpretation of research done in the past, should be based on a new perspective; a perspective that uses the scientific method to effect advances in society, rather than to subjugate and dehumanize (Garcia, Blackwell, Williams and Simpkins, 1969)."

What is needed are ethical guidelines for conducting research on "culturally different peoples." These guidelines should be written in conjunction with representatives of the various culturally different groups, and should be based on a thorough review of the scope and effects of cultural ethnocentrism in the social sciences.

The guidelines should be issued by the various professional associations in the social sciences and in the field of education. There should be strict sanctions for violations of these guidelines. If the guidelines are to work, the government, the largest sponsors of such research, must cease to fund research projects of a culturally ethnocentric nature. Private foundations, which are regulated by the government, must also participate. The government and professional associations should use their influence (certification, monetary support) on the academic community to affect the training of future researchers.

4

Reading and Black Non-Mainstream Students

The Problem

If non-mainstream children wish to make their way successfully in mainstream society, it is necessary that they learn standard American English. In a complex technological, highly impersonal society such as the United States of America, a great deal of information must be shared by means of the printed word. The ability to read well is a prerequisite for navigating one's way through such a society. Without the acquisition of basic reading skills, the probability of having a happy, productive life, free from the crippling cycle of poverty and frustration is low indeed.

Those persons who do not possess basic functional reading abilities—with a few, a very few exceptions—are relegated to a caste system. They become the people least equipped to cope with a complex, rapidly changing society.

Many economic, social and cultural avenues are closed to non-readers and poor readers. When people learn of their illiteracy, they generally consider it to be symptomatic of the low intelligence. This society places a heavy stigma on illiteracy. The illiterate person is considered to be dull, ignorant, backward, narrow and uneducable. Even worse, the illiterate person often comes to consider himself/herself to be all these things and more.

The illiterate person will frequently give up all attempts at formal learning because he or she has internalized the stigma attached to illiteracy.

The illiterate person in a highly literate, technological, achievement-oriented society is hanging by a thin thread practically and psychologically. The person's ego must constantly defend against tremendous feelings and perceptions of inadequacy. As an adjustment, or ego defense, the illiterate often learns to engage in avoidance behavior. He or she often avoids school and educated people because both tend to elicit feelings of anxiety and frustration—feelings of failure and inadequacy.

It is no accident that reading instruction constitutes one of the highest priorities in American education. A school system's reading scores serve as indicators of the academic health of the system. Few indictments of a school system are considered more damning than pupils' low achievement in reading. Many school superintendents have discovered that their job security is directly or indirectly related to how their school system ranks in comparison with national reading norms.

Yet in this country—the most technologically advanced in the world—the reading problem is of frightening proportions. The headline of a recent article read, "Study shows more than one-fifth of U.S. adults functionally illiterate in today's society."

Black non-mainstream students, often referred to as Black inner-city students, represent a reading problem of even greater magnitude. They come from families that are poorer than the general population and that are considerably lower in formal educational attainment. They possess a culture, language and set of experiences that are different from the general population. And to complicate things, they must, for the most part, attend schools that are not prepared and/or willing to use the students' culture, language or experiences in an educational manner.

Their problems are even further complicated by the assumptions made concerning students, which underlie the educational philosophy of schools in this country. It is mistakenly assumed that all students are, or should be, similar to the "idealized White mainstream, normative student." If Black non-mainstream students differ from the normative student by not responding to the methods of instruction and material in a similar manner, their abilities are suspect. They are frequently labeled and stigmatized as "educationally retarded," "culturally deprived," and "linguistically impoverished." This labeling occurs with little or no regard for the fact that the standard of comparison is schools designed to accommodate the culture, language, learning and life styles of White mainstream students.

Today, it is not uncommon for seventh and eighth grade Black non-mainstream students to score at the second and third grade level on standardized reading tests. It is also not uncommon for Black non-mainstream students to finish high school reading below the fifth grade level. The underachievement of Black non-mainstream students has become so widespread that it is no longer necessary to present the statistics of failure. The emphasis today is no longer on documenting the reality of the problem, but on finding its causes and creating ways to remediate its effects.

Educators, acting on advice based on so-called "hard data" from social scientists, have looked to Black students and the Black community in general for the causes of Black students' academic underachievement. The prevailing hypothesis among educators and social scientists is that there is something wrong with Black students. Whether one hypothesizes that it is heredity, i.e. in the children's genetic makeup; or in their environment, i.e., in their culture, language and family structure, the hypothesis is still the same—there is something wrong with Black students. The most frequently alleged causes for the academic failure of Black students are the students themselves and the Black community.

An Alternative Hypothesis for the Underachievement of Black Students

Let us, for a moment, explore a feasible, rival, alternative hypothesis: The causes for the underachievement of Black students lie not in the students nor in the Black community, but in the ethnocentric nature of the dominant society and its educational institutions.

> "If Black people are not achieving in today's educational system, it seems logical to believe that it is not their language (or culture) but the fact that they are Black (Covington, 1973)."

Such an alternative hypothesis should consider the following:

1) African American Language;
2) misconceptions of teachers;
3) the traditional approach of teaching Black children to read; and
4) the mismatch in the instructional system.

A great deal of time and energy is wasted in classrooms around the country trying to program out well-learned verbal behavior in Black students' vernacular. This occurs despite the fact that there exists no empirical evidence to support the popular notion that certain languages are superior to other languages, or that one dialect of a language may be impoverished with respect to another.

> "Yet in no sense is there any empirical evidence to support such notions as language A is "impoverished"

vis-a-vis language B, or that dialect X of language C is "impoverished" with respect to dialect Y of language C; i.e., that the grammar and vocabulary of X is some diminished subset of the grammar and vocabulary of Y. Such notions are meaningless, for the grammars of X and Y are simply equal sets that intersect in vast and important ways (O'Neil, 1971)."

Yet in the case of Black non-mainstream children the notion persists that the phonology, lexicon and syntax of their dialect is a restricted, illogical, poorly constructed imitation of the mainstream American dialect of English. William Labov, one of this country's most respected linguists, summarizes some of the popular misconceptions:

"Negro children from the ghetto area are said to receive little verbal stimulation, to hear very little well-formed language and as a result are impoverished in their means of verbal expression. They cannot speak complete sentences, do not know the names of common objects, cannot form concepts or convey logical thoughts (Labov, 1969)."

These misconceptions have no basis in linguistics. They are based on racial, social class and stylistic preferences. Their roots are to be found in the ethnocentric manner in which this country views language differences and the misleading information that has been disseminated by social scientists. Labov goes on to say:

"Unfortunately, these notions are based upon the work of educational psychologists who know very little about language and even less about Negro children. The concept of verbal deprivation has no basis in social reality. In fact, Negro children in urban ghettos

receive a great deal of verbal stimulation, hear more
well-formed sentences than middle class children, and
participate fully in a highly verbal culture. They have
the same basic vocabulary, possess the same capacity
for learning, and use logic (Labov, 1969)."

Many Black students speak a variety of English sufficiently
different from the mainstream American dialect of English to
be considered a separate linguistic system with its own independent structure and logic. African American Language (sometimes referred to as Ebonics, Black vernacular, Black idiom and
Black non-standard English) is a cohesive, well developed, rule-
governed, complex linguistic system closely related to, while in
many ways different from, the mainstream American dialect of
English.

It is important to note that many speakers of African American Language (AAL), for the most part (quantitatively and quali-
tatively), have more standard than non-standard forms in their
speech. The similarities between AAL and standard English are
much greater than their differences. However, AAL speakers
use more non-standard terms than other groups and they also use
different forms which are absent from the speech of other groups.
An example of these different forms is the absence of the linking
verb, as in "he late," and in the use of the distinctive "be," as in
"He be late."

Speakers of African American Language (AAL) often have
trouble reading Standard Written English (SWE) because they
do not see their speech and cultural practices reflected there. AAL
(primarily a spoken language) and SWE each allows constructions not common in the other. For example, in AAL, in certain
types of sentences—e.g., equative constructions—a verb is not
obligatory, as in "She a big girl now." With equative construc-

tions in SWE, however, the verb is obligatory. Thus, SWE would be "She is a big girl now."

Discrepancies between oral and written language patterns affect sound-to-letter correspondences, grammar, vocabulary, and styles of statement. The following discussion is intended to suggest that differences between a spoken language and a written one may be related to reading problems.

Grammar and Sounds

When a person reads, his or her speech is involved in recognizing the printed symbol, decoding the printed form to a spoken form, and assigning meaning to what is decoded. Every reader faces the general problem of irregularities of sound-to-letter correspondences in English. African American Language speakers, however, bear the added burden of encountering in Standard Written English patterns not found in their speech. For example, there is a phonological (sound) rule in African American Language which allows a weakening or deletion of the final consonant or consonant cluster in a word. This weakening or elimination process often creates homonyms not found in Standard English. Examples of such homonyms are: find-fine, cold-coal, told-toll, floor-flow, door-dough, and parents-pants. These African American Language homonyms are not homonyms in spoken Standard English. Readers who cannot "hear" and decode the written word into their familiar linguistic framework may find the written patterns complicated and confusing. When this happens, some readers lose confidence in the printed symbol and become discouraged with their attempts to read.

The grammatical system of African American Language has a number of differences from Standard Written English. For example, where verbs in SWE indicate past, present, or future tense,

AAL has an aspectual verb system whereby a speaker can indicate that an action or event is occurring at the moment, or, by contrast, occurs on an intermittent, habitual basis over time. In the sentence, "That boy, he talking a lot," the absence of "be" indicates that the boy happens to be talking a lot at the moment. Whether or not he also talks a lot on a regular basis cannot be determined from this sentence. To convey that meaning, one would have to say, "That boy, he be talking a lot." Here the inclusion of "be" indicates that the boy talks a lot on a habitual basis—although at the moment the statement is made, the boy may not even be talking. Some African American Language examples of this aspectual verb pattern and their Standard Written English equivalents are given below.

African American Language (AAL)	Standard Written English (SWE)
She on time to school.	Today she is at school on time.
She be on time to school.	She is usually at school on time.
She say she don't be on time to school.	She said she is usually not at school on time.
He real hungry.	He is very hungry now.
He be hungry when we get there.	He is usually hungry when we get there.

There are other differences between the grammar of AAL and that of SWE. For example, consider the way AAL speakers indicate that an event or action was not only completed but done so in the distant past. The AAL speaker will put stress on the verb "been," as in "I BEEN finish that book," for SWE "I finished that book a long time ago." Some other AAL patterns are given below:

Pattern	AAL	SWE
Future *be*	She be here in a minute	She will be here in a minute.
Possessive (no –*s* morpheme, meaning by context)	That was Mr. Johnson store.	That was Mr. Johnson's store.
Plural (no –*s* morpheme, meaning by context)	Two girl gone to get it.	Two girls went to get it.
Present Tense, 3rd singular verbs (no –*s* morpheme)	His brother look the same way.	His brother looks the same way.
	She do the same thang every day.	She does the same thing every day.
	Mary have twin brother.	Mary has twin brothers.
Future *gõ* (nasalized vowel)	He was gon tell his momma "Bye."	He was going to tell his momma "Bye."
Future *be*	She be here in a minute	She will be here in a minute.
Existential *It*	It's a lot of people live in that house.	There are a lot of people living in that house.
Multiple Negation	I can't never get no help with nothin round here.	I can never get any help with anything around here.

Pattern	AAL	SWE
Don't/Ain't but for limited negation (=*only*)	Don't but two people know what really happen.	Only two people know what really happened.
Negative Inversion	Don't nobody don't know God can't tell me nothin.	Anybody who doesn't God know cannot tell me anything.
Stay for Persistent Activity	He stay on the phone.	He uses the telephone quite a lot.
Past Tense (no *-ed* morpheme, meaning by context	We look for him everywhere but never did find him.	We looked for him everywhere but never did find him.
Perfective *done*,	He done lost his book.	He has lost his book
(unstressed) *been*,	They been there a long time.	They have been there a long time.
done been	They done been sitting out there a whole hour.	They have been sitting out there an entire hour.
Pronominal Apposition, for emphasis.	That teacher, she be hollin a lot.	That teacher is mean and yells a lot.
Vowel /I/ + *ng* or *nk* realized as *ang, ank*.	That's the thang I don't like about it.	That's the thing I don't like about it.
	They some sanging Sistas.	They are some singing Sisters.
	He thank he bad.	He thinks he is powerful.

Pattern	AAL	SWE
Static locatives, presentatives	There go my momma nem in the front row.	There are my mother and others in the front row.
	Here go my list of words.	Here is my list of words.

The above discussion and lists are not meant to be exhaustive. There are numerous other differences between the phonological and syntactical (grammatical) systems of AAL and SWE which are too extensive to present here. One thing to keep in mind, however, is that no single AAL speaker uses all of the different patterns. Nor does any single speaker use all of the patterns all of the time.

Vocabulary, Idioms, and Folk Sayings

In addition to phonological and syntactical differences between African American Language and Standard Written English, there are differences in vocabulary and styles of speaking. Some words function as intensifiers in AAL. For example, we hear, "He a cold dealer" (with "cold" pronounced as "coal"). If the AAL speaker really wanted to stress the adjective "cold," the speaker would use "stone" to intensify the coldness: "He a stone cold dealer." A stone cold dealer may be a person who lacks compassion, a person who is very good at dealing cards, or a person who drives a hard bargain. Even though an AAL speaker may know the aforementioned possibilities for decoding the meaning of the statement, he or she nevertheless has to determine the meaning called for in the context where the statement is used. Hence the emphasis in *Bridge 2* on vocabulary practice or word bridging in sentence-story context.

Many idioms and folk sayings used by AAL speakers have been around for a long time and are passed on from one generation to the next. For example, the current popular terms "homey" and "homeboy/homegirl" are variations on the terms "homes" and "home," which hark back at least half a century and were used, as "homey" is used today, to refer to someone from the same neighborhood or with a similar background who was presumed to be a kindred spirit. "A hard head make a soft behind" is an old proverbial folk saying that warns about negative outcomes if one refuses to listen to and follow sound advice. The related idiom "hardheaded" is used to describe a person who is stubborn and who refuses to heed the lessons that have been gained from experience.

In African American peer groups, innovation in figurative uses of language is highly valued, and idioms and folk expressions are constantly created. However, this is—the figurative language of literary pieces read in school. Some AAL vocabulary terms and figurative expressions and their meanings are shown below:

(AAL)	(SWE)
She on time to school.	Today she is at school on time.
Cleaner than the Board of Health	Well-dressed
They be half-steppin.	Their performance is usually inadequate.
Nose open	Vulnerably in love
He don't know what time it is.	Not knowledgeable, uninformed
Selling woof ("wolf") tickets	Bluffing
Not wrapped too tight	Unstable, out of touch with reality
Hawk and his brother, Joe	Chilly, powerful wind, extreme cold
Call somebody outa they name	Insult, offend
Denzel Washington is too fine.	Denzel Washington is very handsome.

(AAL)	(SWE)
Know what I'm sayin?	Do you understand me?
I feel you.	I completely understand what you are saying, and I sympathize with you.
You a day late and a dollar short.	Unprepared, disorganized. You have failed to live up to your or responsibilities.

Conclusion

The language of African Americans has been the subject of numerous research studies, dating as far back as James A. Harrison's *Negro English*, published in the journal *Anglia* in 1884. In the first half of the Twentieth Century, there were pioneering studies by anthropologist Melville Herskovits (*Myth of the Negro Past*, 1941) and linguist Lorenzo D. Turner (*Africanisms in the Gullah Dialect*, 1949). In the 1960's and '70's, linguists conducted extensive analyses of the full range of African American Language—the phonology, syntax, vocabulary, rhetorical styles, discourse modes, proverb use, and folk expressions. Some scholars have emphasized the African language background (e.g., Holloway and Vass, *The African Heritage of American English*, 1993). Other scholars focus on the connection between AAL and Creole languages of the Caribbean (e.g., Rickford, *African American Vernacular English*, 1999). The voluminous body of research on AAL has not only demonstrated the systematic nature of the language, but also its integral relationship to the history, culture, world view, values and life experiences of people of African descent in America. The background on African American Language presented here is merely a snapshot of this total, pervasive communication system, which is used by all segments of the African American community.

Teachers who would like to read more about AAL and about the relationship between language and education might wish to consult any of the books mentioned above and/or any of the following: *Ebonics and Language Education of African Ancestry Students*, edited by Clinton Crawford (2001); *Spoken Soul*, by John and Russell Rickford (2000; winner of an American Book Award); *Black Talk: Words and Phrases from the Hood to the Amen Corner* and *Talkin That Talk: Language, Culture and Education in African America*, by Geneva Smitherman (2000); *Out of the Mouths of Slaves: African American Language and Educational Malpractice*, by John Baugh (1999); *Making the Connection: Language and Academic Achievement Among African American Students*, edited by Carolyn Adger, Donna Christian and Orlando Taylor (1999); *Africanisms in Afro-American Language Varieties*, edited by Salikoko S. Mufwene (1993); *Black and White Styles in Conflict* by Thomas Kochman (1981); *The Bantu Speaking Heritage of the United States*, by Winifred Vass (1979); *Black English: Its History and Usage in the United States* by J.L. Dillard (1972); *Language in the Inner City* by William Labov (1972).

To the extent that your students' linguistic-cultural style differs from that of Standard Written English, it is a potential source of reading problems for them. You will have to determine the extent of the problem for different students. Having some background knowledge of the language of the students you teach should help you to better understand and cope with their reading difficulties (Simpkins, Smitherman, Stalling, 2001).

Misconceptions of Teaching

The absence of African American Language features from most instructional reading materials, and the ability or reluctance of most teachers to use these features in a positive educational manner in the classroom contribute to the academic difficulties of the

Black non-mainstream student.

Practically all teachers emerge from backgrounds that can be categorized as mainstream, or middle class. Even if the teachers came from a non-mainstream background, they are generally mainstream in their cultural and social orientation as a function of the training and socialization they have undergone en route to becoming a teacher. (There are numerous exceptions, but they are exceptions rather than the rule.)

In part, the educational difficulties encountered by Black non-mainstream children in learning to read are due to the kind of language and experiences that they bring with them when they enter school. Many of these children have different cultural and social backgrounds from their teachers. The environment in which these children live and learn is also, in most instances, different. Teachers seldom have the opportunity in their professional training to study the environment in which these children develop; and when they do, teachers are generally focused on weaknesses and assumed deficiencies, rather than on strengths and differences.

There is a tendency for teachers to assume that all children are, or at least should be very much alike—very much like mainstream normative children. The tendency is to assume that if Black non-mainstream children do not have the normative behaviors and learning experience when they enter school, they have not learned anything. Many teachers overlook the fact that a great deal of learning takes place in the Black non-mainstream children's environment before they enter school, and concurrently while they are in school.

"It is not unusual to see a five- or six-year old Black inner-city child, labeled (by the schools) culturally deprived and educable retarded, mastering learning behaviors of a much greater complexity in his environment than those he has failed to learn in the school. These same children often have the sophistication of thirteen-

and fourteen-year old White middle class youths. They often take care of younger siblings, shop, cook, clean house and display a highly sophisticated language development in their vernacular (Simpkins, 1969)."

Most Black non-mainstream children experience very few or no learning difficulties prior to the onset of formal schooling. Yet after they enter school, the longer they stay, the further behind they fall. Outside school, in the natural environment again, the children experience few or no learning difficulties.

Whatever learning difficulties present themselves for the Black student in the classroom, all such difficulties are resolved when he or she hits the streets. Educators must ask why is learning on the street so efficient? Why has learning in the classroom been so inefficient? How can education, as a process, benefit from observing how children learn outside of school? (Kochman, 1969).

Skills learned outside of school may come into conflict with the skills that the school is attempting to teach. A prime example of that conflict is in the area of language. The language skills necessary for Black non-mainstream children to successfully negotiate their way through their environment outside the school differ from the language skills required for ultimate success in the schools (Simpkins, 1973).

These out-of-school verbal skills are often considered by teachers to inhibit formal classroom learning. They are seldom recognized as legitimate verbal abilities and thus they are seldom utilized in teaching reading. Non-mainstream Black children with highly proficient verbal skills in their natural environment are discouraged from using these verbal skills because they are considered by teachers to be vulgar, backward, irrelevant, and destructive to learning in the classroom. They are considered to constitute "learning the wrong way." Teachers often fail to realize that there is no such thing as learning "the wrong way" when what is learned fosters adaptive behavior in the learner's natural environment. They try to program out well-learned verbal skills and competencies in order to facilitate formal "correct learning." All too often the effects of such well meaning efforts result in the exact opposite of that intended by the teachers.

The Traditional Approach to Teaching Black Children to Read

Traditionally, in this country, teaching Black children to read consisted of giving the children basal readers about White children looking and seeing each other running and playing with their dog, Spot. When the children passed this stage, they were introduced to the joys of reading about White mainstream children who lived in big white houses on tree-lined streets with carpet-like green lawns. And, of course, the children would read about father who was a big White man in a business suit and mother who had nothing to do all day but bake cookies and cakes, shop and clean the big white house.

The rationale for using such instructional materials was that the average American child either came from a similar mainstream background or was at least familiar with such a background. It was thought that this familiarity held the children's attention and made it easier for them to read and comprehend.

Mismatch in the Instructional System

In the case of Black non-mainstream children, the mainstream frame of reference of the reading instruction materials was unfamiliar and did not represent their reality. There existed a mismatch in terms of the children's culture, language, experiences and interests. What this mismatch represented was a massive breakdown in the instructional system.

The major variables in an instructional system are the child, the teacher and the developer of instructional materials. The children were mismatched with teachers and developers of instructional materials in terms of sociocultural and linguistic backgrounds.

> Learning to read is contingent upon the child's speech skills and the social environment in which he uses them... When the child, the teacher and the developer of instructional materials share a common social and linguistic background, the effectiveness of reading materials need not suffer if many social and linguistic aspects of instruction are left tacit. However, when social and linguistic backgrounds vary from child to teacher to developer, then the instructional system must take into account the background of the child. Otherwise, ineffective reading instruction will result (Legum, William and Lee, 1969).

Cognitively, due to the mismatch in the instructional system, the task of learning to read is much greater for non-mainstream children than for their mainstream counterparts. The Black non-mainstream student must not only learn to decode and comprehend written words, he must also take on the additional task of translating them into his familiar language and sociocultural frame of reference.

> This presents him with an almost insurmountable obstacle since the written words frequently do not go together in any pattern that is familiar or meaningful to him. He is baffled by this confrontation with (1) a new language with its new syntax; (2) a necessity to learn the meaning of graphic symbols; and (3) a vague, or not so vague (depending on the cultural and linguistic sophistication of the teacher) sense that there is some-

thing terribly wrong with his language (Baratz, J., 1969).

The traditional basal readers have disappeared from most schools. Black faces have begun to appear in some instructional reading materials and some of the readers feature stories about Black people. But what has not disappeared is the mismatch in the instructional system. It is as true today as it was forty years ago—reading instructional materials do not reflect the culture, language and interests of Black non-mainstream children.

> Many linguists, aware of the fact that the Black non-mainstream child when reading, faces the difficult task of not only decoding an unfamiliar syntax (grammar) but also must perform the additional task of translating the material into his familiar language AAL code, have begun to advocate the design and use of instructional materials that are culturally and linguistically specific. They suggest that dialect readers be used as a starting point in the reading process and later transition to reading materials be used to assist the learner to read Standard English materials (Baratz, 1969, Steward, 1960, Leaveton, 1973, Labov, 1995, Rickford, 1995, Smitherman, 1996).

In 1965, Steward translated into African American vernacular Clement Clarke Moore's poem, "A Visit From St. Nicholas" (The Night Before Christmas). It read:

> It's the night before Christmas, and here in our house
> it ain't nothing moving, not even no mouse.
>
> There go we-all stockings, hanging high up off the floor.
>
> So Santa Claus can full them up, if he walk in through the door.

Steward stated that, while he was working on a draft of the poem, a 12-year-old girl who lived in the inner-city read the poem. The girl was experiencing reading problems in school, but read aloud the African American Language version of the poem with no difficulty. In addition, she read it with fluency and intonation. But when asked to read the standard English version of the poem, she experienced great difficulty; she stumbled and staggered through the poem.

This lead Steward to hypothesize that the difficulty in reading experienced by inner-city Black children can be attributed to "structure interference between the grammatical patterns of their 'nonstandard dialect' and that of standard English." After examining the effectiveness of dialectal reading materials, Leaveton (1973) came to similar conclusions.

The Bridge Reading Program, according to Patricia A. Young (1999), "answered the call to assist in the education of inner city Black children. The designers....created a skill-based reading program that included a linguistic and cultural context and participatory activities. This reading program sought to empower students, support their language, support their culture, and teach them how to read." (The Bridge Reading Program will be analyzed to illustrate the development of a curriculum based on a Cultural Difference Model later in this book.)

Young goes on to ask the question, "Are dialect readers the answer to educating speakers of a dialect?" Labov believes that, "The initial success of the *Bridge Program* in its primary function to improve reading scores is sufficient to warrant careful attention and a search for ways of developing its basic principles further. Its development has far-reaching implications for similar programs" (Labov, 1995).

5

The Cross-Cultural Approach
to Reading Education

The Cross-Cultural Approach to Education is a pedagogical approach designed to accommodate the culture and language of Black non-mainstream students. It is an educational approach which attempts to bridge the void that exists between the learning that takes place in the Black non-mainstream home and community and the learning that Black students are expected to acquire in schools. An overriding theoretical, philosophical, and political consideration of the Cross-Cultural Approach is that any educational program for Black students must be part of, and sympathetic to, the students' culture, language, experiences and interests.

A second major consideration is the importance of language in the educational program. The culture and experiences of students are reflected in their language. They speak the language of those with whom they identify and those who are most meaningful to them. AAVE, aside from being central to human communication and identity, has been the convenient whipping boy of programs which have sought to normalize Black non-mainstream students under the guise of remedying a defective language and culture.

A basic premise of the Cross-Cultural Approach is that the repertoire of language skills and competencies brought to school by Black non-mainstream children can and should be used to facilitate new learning. This approach represents an attempt to utilize the learning that Black non-mainstream children have experienced outside of school. The strategy of this approach is to engage the students by using as a starting point in the learning process, the verbal behavior of the students in their familiar cultural context.

In educational pedagogy there is almost universal belief in the Dewey axiom, "Start where the child is." In the field of linguistics, this axiom becomes a battle cry, "Begin with the child's cultural-linguistic knowledge and experiences as a educational foundation upon which to build." The Cross-Cultural Approach views language as the common denominator between what students know and what they are expected to learn. It embraces the presupposition that reading, or any other subject matter, can be best taught by beginning with the verbal behavior that is available to learners, and utilizing instructional materials that incorporate language with which the learners already have phonetic, lexical, syntactical and cultural familiarity. This familiarity then forms the cultural context for the learners. It assists the learners in comprehending concepts that otherwise may appear strange and confusing.

Cognitive Concerns of the Cross-Cultural Approach

It is assumed in the Cross-Cultural Approach that Black non-mainstream children have the same cognitive apparatus and abilities as mainstream children; that differences in academic performance occur because their cognitive apparatus is differentially triggered by the cultural context. The differential triggering of their cognitive apparatus causes learning to be more effective for these students "in the streets" than in the classroom. Similarly, as with the phenomenon that occurs in reading, the students must perform an additional cognitive operation in order to grasp many concepts taught in the schools. They must translate incoming conceptual material into their familiar cultural context.

If one studies, as this author has, the behavior of Black non-mainstream students at the entering college level, one will observe evidence of this phenomenon. The following is one of many similar observations made by the author:

"Hey man, what was he talking 'bout? I ain't understand a word of that stuff. I was completely lost. And everybody else look like they knew what was going on. I'm gon drop this class; that shit is hard as Chinese algebra."

The other student responded, "No man, hang on in. That stuff is light. It's just the way he talk that make it seem hard. Dig it, what the dude was trying to say was..."

After the fellow student finished translating the lecture, the first student said, "Damn man, why didn't he say that in the first place? Them White folks always be trying to make stuff hard."

In the above exchange, one student was able to translate the conceptual material into the familiar cultural context and was therefore able to help his fellow student understand the concepts.

I once taught research methodology at a major urban university with a class composed entirely of Black undergraduates. They found it difficult to comprehend the meaning and function of many of the concepts. The readings were, to use their words, "Greek to them." After several unsuccessful attempts to explain the concepts in standard mainstream English, I began lecturing in African American Language (in the students' familiar cultural context). The following is taken from a taped lecture given to that class:

Okay, say you got two Brothers—Brother A and Brother B. For the purpose of illustration, we will consider Brother A out experimental group and Brother

B our control group. Now, these two Brothers are hitting on this here stone foxy lady. Now, we the researchers. We a research team and this is our experiment. Now what we wanta know is, which one of the Brothers got the best rap, which one got the strongest game. Can you dig it?

Now, our independent variable under study is the Brothers' rap, and our dependent variable is getting over. You know, making a hit—getting next to the sweet young foxy lady. You all got that? The independent variable—the presumed cause—is the Brothers' rap. And our dependent variable—the presumed effect—is getting over with the fox. Everybody got that? All right, now we cooking. We gon make some sense of this stuff.

Now, we wanta make sure that the Brother who gets over gets over 'cause of his rap—our independent variable under study. So we gotta be controlling for some things. One of the Brothers just may be over, quiet as it's kept, 'cause he got some long green, some heavy bread. And that would have nothing at all to do with his rap. Now would it? Right on. Did everybody hear that? That's an extraneous variable or an unwanted variable. It's also an independent variable that could effect the outcome, 'cause long green show 'nough can help you get over.

Can you think of some more extraneous or unwanted variables that are also independent variables that we need to be controlling for? Did everybody hear that? The Brother may get over 'cause he super fly. So we gotta be controlling for rags, for dress. Can you think of any more? Right on. You got it. We gotta be controlling for the Brother's ride, and the Brother's looks.

The Brother may have a bad set of wheels and get over. And he may be a good-looking dude and get over on his looks. A whole lot of you Sisters like them pretty boys. And one more thing—the Brother may get over 'cause he's a professor. You know, he be teaching research methodology at the University and that may impress the fox. So we gotta be controlling for his gig.

Okay, now that we done generate a list of extraneous, or unwanted, variables that are also independent variables that can effect the outcome of our experiment, what we gon do to control them? Speak up. I can't hear you. Did everyone hear that? We gotta randomize. I see you been reading the book. That's good. Randomization is the best thing to do to control extraneous variables. Except in this case. We can't randomize 'cause we only got a N of two, Brother A and Brother B. But if we had more subjects in our experiment and control groups, that would be the best thing to do. 'Cause then we could just assume that both groups would be equal of everything. So we gotta go the next best thing. Can anybody run it down to me what that is? Right on, Sister. I see you been dealing with the book too. Did everybody hear her? We gotta match. We gotta match the Brothers on all the other independent variables that might possibly effect the outcome of our experiment. And that's all the ones we listed, except our independent variables under study—the Brother's rap.

So what we gotta do is make sure that Brother A and Brother B both got the same amount of bread, the same ride, just about the same looks, rags, gigs and all that good stuff. We do that so that if one of the

Brothers get over, we can say, with a fair amount of certainty, that he got over because of our independent variable under study—his rap. Can you dig it? Good question. What if none of the Brothers get over? Well, then we say that there wasn't no significant difference in their rap. They both struck out.

Although Campbell, Stanley and Kerlinger (the authors of the two texts used in the class) would probably cringe at the above lecture, the students found it extremely helpful. After a series of lectures illustrating the concepts of research methodology in the students' familiar cultural context, the students found it easier to read the assigned texts. They were able to demonstrate on exams, in standard mainstream English, basic knowledge of the concepts and details of the course.

The problems encountered by these students are not isolated amusing instances; they are representative of the difficulties experienced by a great many Black non-mainstream students at all levels of the school system throughout this country. Many students sit through classes confused, never understanding the concepts that are being presented. Many students manage to pass classes, some with high grades, by mimicking back the instructor's lectures and the contents of their texts without ever understanding the concepts.

Rivers (1969) describes the organization of cognitive patterns in Black non-mainstream students. He suggests that in many instances standard English, in the context of mainstream culture, does not signal or activate the Black child's linguistic conceptual systems to the extent that systematic transformations are involved to produce appropriate cognitive responses. He theorizes that the child's "communication intake gates" may not be fully activated by the stimulus properties of standard mainstream English.

The underlying academic problem of Black mainstream students appears to be a mismatch in the two languages and the instructional system. Although most teachers do not possess the knowledge and ability to eliminate the additional cognitive operations that many of these students have to perform in translating from standard English to the African American Language, instructional materials can be developed in the students' familiar cultural context. The Cross-Cultural Approach addresses the problems encountered by non-mainstream students which pertain to the mismatch in the instructional system.

Teaching-Learning Strategies of the Cross-Cultural Approach

There are two teaching-learning strategies in the Cross-Cultural Approach in teaching reading in the *Bridge Program*. These two educational strategies are called Associative Bridging and Peer Control. Both strategies are designed to accommodate the culture and language of Black non-mainstream students. They are designed to bridge the void which exists between learning in the Black community and learning in the schools.

Associative Bridging is the general educational strategy which underlies the entire Cross-Cultural Approach. It is reflected in almost every aspect of the Approach. Peer Control is a specific educational strategy designed to give students control over the learning process and to accommodate the oral tradition of the Black community.

Associative Bridging

The Associative Bridging strategy (Simpkins, 1973), broadly speaking, is a restatement and extension of the Dewey axiom—

start where the children are and take them to where you would like them to be in a series of steps, utilizing their cultural-linguistic knowledge as an educational foundation. It is the process of going from the familiar to the less familiar in a series of steps, associating the familiar elements with the less familiar elements. The familiar is African American Language in the context of Black non-mainstream culture. The less familiar is standard mainstream English in the context of mainstream culture.

Associative Bridging uses African American Language as a starting point (assuming that the students are most familiar with this language population and possess their most accomplished verbal skills in it). This method seeks to improve the students' reading ability by first teaching them in their dialect, and then extending that learning via a series of steps to the standard mainstream English. Reading in the mainstream dialect is thus taught as an extension of reading in the student's familiar dialect. In this way, Black non-mainstream English serves as a springboard from which to move to the presentation of standard mainstream English.

Two Language Populations

If one accepts that the language spoken by Black non-mainstream children is systematic, logical, rule-governed, and by no means a primitive underdeveloped version of standard English, then one can conceptualize two different language populations. These two different language populations can be labeled (1) African American Language, and (2) standard mainstream English (Simpkins, 1973).

As mentioned in Chapter 3, Black non-mainstream children often bring to school a great deal of well-learned verbal behavior. For example, African American Language is an expressive mode of communication which draws heavily on metaphoric language (Holt, 1971). When teachers attempt to teach Black non-mainstream students metaphors or figurative language in the classroom, few teachers utilize the metaphoric quality of their Black students' language. Instead, they try to teach a different figurative language, often using what is to the students, a strange vocabulary, embedded in strange syntax, to form strange and confusing metaphors.

These same students who failed to learn what a metaphor is and how to use and understand figurative language have been heard to say, once they hit the streets, things like, "The teacher didn't cut me no slack. She was steadily on my case. This school stuff is a strain on the brain. But that's okay, I'm just gon lay in the cut." On the streets, within the Black non-mainstream language population, Black students use and understand a profusion of metaphors and richly figurative language.

Bridging the Two Language Populations

African American Language and standard mainstream English often blend together as one language population in the speech of Black children. This is a natural phenomenon—the children's language is in fact a mixture of standard mainstream English with non-standard features. The children do not make discriminations between the two language populations in their speech. It is hypothesized that in order to bridge the two language populations the children must begin to acquire fine and gross discriminations between the two language populations (Simpkins, 1973). The fine discriminations contain elements of language such as syntax and lexicon, but not phonology. The gross discriminations are life styles, values, and plots. The fine and gross discriminations are achieved systematically by contrasting the elements of the two language populations.

The student, for example, progresses from reading materials and accompanying skill exercises written in African American Language to reading materials and skill exercises written in a transition form. The transition form consists of a series of steps which constitute the bridge between the two language populations. In addition, the instructional materials in the transition form use a blend or combination of both language populations. In some of the transition forms, the combination or blend is weighted toward standard mainstream English, while in others, it is weighted toward Black non-mainstream English. The student proceeds from the transition form to materials and skill exercises written in standard mainstream English, thus completing the progression from the familiar to the less familiar. In the progression, the content of the skill exercises varies, while the concepts (skills) are held relatively constant.

Both dialects are presented to the student on an equal footing. Careful attention is paid to eradicating the negative value connotations that the schools, teachers and the dominant society, in general, have placed on Black non-standard English.

Associative Bridging can be conceptualized as the methodology for spanning the two language populations. By making the two language populations distinct, the students can learn reading and associated reading skills in their familiar dialect; then, through a series of transitional steps, they can generalize this learning to the less familiar dialect. Once the students have experienced success in learning in their familiar language population and are made aware of the similarities and differences of the properties of the two language populations, they can transfer this learning to the less familiar language population. This process rectifies the mismatch in the instructional system for Black non-mainstream students and provides the methodology for assisting the students to make the appropriate linguistic and cognitive translations.

Peer Control

Peer Control is a specific teaching-learning strategy of the Cross-Cultural Approach. It is an oral reading procedure designed to give students control over the learning process.

The "Equality of Educational Opportunity Survey" (Coleman, 1966) examined three expressions of student attitude and motivation which were believed to be closely related to academic achievement. The first was interest in learning. The second attitudinal variable examined was the student's self-concept. The third variable examined was labeled by the report as "sense of control of the environment." The report defined sense of control of the environment in the following manner:

> For children from disadvantaged groups, achievement or lack of achievement, appears closely related to what they believe about their environment: whether they believe the environment will respond to reasonable efforts, or whether they believe it is instead merely random or immovable. In different words, it appears that children from advantaged groups assume that the environment will respond if they are able enough to affect it. Children from disadvantaged groups do not make this assumption, but in many cases assume that nothing they do can affect the environment—it will give benefits or withhold them, but not as a consequence of their own actions (Coleman, 1966).

The sense of control of the environment variable, as stated in the introduction to this book, proved to be the most important variable for predicting the achievement level of Black students. It accounted for approximately three times as much test variance for Black students as for their White counterparts. It was considerably stronger in its relation to achievement than any of the family background factors. Altschuler (1973) suggests that the relationship between sense of control of the environment and achievement results from the psychological consequences of oppression.

The painful consequences of this institutionalized oppression of children do not stop with induced poorer self-image, lower self-confidence, and less belief that they can alter their fate. To the degree children internalize the belief that they are somehow inadequate (instead of oppressed), they also do poorly in school. In other words, if children believe they cannot control their own fate, that their efforts make little difference in what happens to them, then they do not make use of, or benefit as much from, the schooling available. It is easy to trace the escalating vicious cycle. With each year of school, minority children fall further behind, aided by mono-racial curricula and biased school standards.

The Coleman study documented the massive pattern of academic failure among Black students in this country's school system. The question that still remains, many years later, is: what can be done? The question is one of policy: How can educational opportunity best be provided? The persistence of the problem and the experience of the last three decades seem to suggest that in order to implement educational opportunity, greater attention must be focused by educators, researchers, and government on providing new methods and materials which accommodate the experiences, realities and needs of Black children.

> If we really want to provide educational opportunity for the ghetto-bound child, these are the kinds of hard issues that will have to be addressed. We'll have to explore whether Negro children have educational needs that are distinctive, whether new methods and materials are required, and if it is possible and desirable to

develop a "black" curriculum, one that is responsive to the reality of the Negro child's existence (Day, 1969).

Kennth B. Clark, one of the pioneers in the struggle for equal educational opportunity in this country, raises similar concerns:

> Some questions which we must now dare to ask and seek to answer as the bases for a new strategy in the assault against the inhumanity of the American system of racial segregation are: (1) Is the present pattern of massive educational inferiority and inefficiency which is found in predominantly Negro schools inherent and inevitable in racially segregated schools? (2) Is there anything which can be done within the Negro schools to raise them to a tolerable level of educational excellence?
>
> If the answer to the first question is yes and to the second question is no, then the continued and intensified assault on the system of segregated schools is justified and should be continued unabated...If, on the other hand, the answers to the above questions are reversed, it would suggest that a shift in strategy and tactics, without giving up the ultimate goals of eliminating the dehumanizing force of racial segregation from American life, would be indicated (Clark, 1968).

It is proposed here that the question to be answered is: In what type of program would Black non-mainstream children best achieve? If the assumption is accepted that Black non-mainstream children with a low sense of control of their environment perceive their environment in a somewhat realistic manner (i.e. the environment is harsh and tends to be immovable; it will give benefits or withhold them, but not necessarily as a consequence of their own action), then it may be concluded that the achievement level of these children will be higher in an environment in which they can control the reinforcements.

Although teachers can do little to provide Black children with greater control of the environment outside the classroom, a great deal can be done within the classroom to provide them with greater control over the reinforcements. Teachers, for example, control the distribution of positive and negative reinforcements. This is accomplished by smiles, frowns, threats, verbal approval or reprimand, and grades. Hammond and Simpkins (1973) point out that teachers often distribute reinforcements on a non-contingent basis. They go on to suggest that those children who are closest to the teachers' mainstream orientations in their speech patterns, values and aspirations receive the lion's share of the positive reinforcement. Silberman (1965) suggests that freedom from the teacher may serve as a positive reinforcer.

Labov et al. (1968) report that the primary influence on the verbal behavior of Black non-mainstream children is the peer group. He recommends that the peer group influence should somehow be made compatible with the implicit requirements of the school.

Kochman (1969) differentiates two distinctive styles of learning operating in Black and White children. These different styles, he suggests, are dictated by their respective cultures. White mainstream children (more accurately, mainstream children in general) tend to learn best via the written channel, by means of tests and papers; whereas Black non-mainstream children tend to learn best via the spoken word, by means of oral-aural communication. Kochman points out that, though the schools give recognition and reinforcement to learning via the written channel by means of tests and papers, little or no scholastic recognition is given for oral expertise, particularly spontaneous oral expertise, which tends to be highly developed in Black culture. This means that there is a mismatch between the value placed on oral expertise inside the classroom and the value placed on it outside the classroom. He strongly suggests that education as a process can benefit from observing how Black non-mainstream children learn outside the classroom and from understanding the role that culture plays in the learning process of these children.

A similar position is taken by Simpkins (1973). He recommends that the implicit requirements of the classroom should be made acceptable with the implicit requirements of the Black non-mainstream child's cultural environment outside the classroom.

Extrapolating from the above, a program model designed to raise achievement levels of Black non-mainstream children with a low sense of control of the environment might include the following:

1) Reinforcers that are controlled by the students rather than the teachers.
2) The influence of the peer group as a major factor in the learning process.
3) Emphasis on learning via the spoken channel via oral-aural communication.

The Peer Control Method

These three points are incorporated into a teaching method called Peer Control (Simpkins, 1973; Simpkins et al., 1974). The full name of this teaching method is Peer Control and Student Feedback Oral Reading Procedure. In addition to the three previously mentioned points, the Peer Control Method also includes the following:

1) Reinforcement is contingent upon the accuracy of the students' response in a manner which leads to the shaping of skillful reading behavior.
2) Knowledge of the correctness or incorrectness of the students' responses is supplied in close temporal relation to the responses by a built-in feedback system.

3) Control of the learning process is turned over to the students on a gradual basis.

Description of the Peer Control Procedures

In the Peer Control procedure, students are assigned by the teacher to small groups. The groups are matched by the teacher as closely as possible in terms of reading proficiency. This practice serves to maximize the probability for equal success on the part of all the participants in the group.

Each student in the group is assigned a number ranging from one to five, depending upon the size of the group. The numbers are randomly assigned by placing them on slips of paper and having each student select one from a receptacle. One number is randomly selected; the student whose number corresponds to the number selected is designated "The Reader." The other students in the group are called "The Correctors."

Each student in the group has an identical copy of a reading selection. The reader's task is to read orally to the group a fixed portion of the reading selection. The task of each Corrector is to read silently along with the Reader, stopping the Reader whenever she recognizes an inappropriate response to the reading selection; i.e. an error. When the Reader is stopped by a Corrector, the error in his reading is pointed out and a correction given. The Reader must then return to the beginning of his portion of the reading selection.

When the Reader successfully completes her portion of the reading selection without being stopped, she then becomes one of the Correctors. The Reader selects another student's number from the receptacle and that student becomes the Reader. This sequence is repeated until each student in the group has completed a turn as the Reader. After the last student in the group has completed his/her turn as the Reader, the numbers are returned by the students to the receptacle and the procedure starts again. The group continually rotates in this manner.

The teacher assigns the portions of the reading selection. She will generally begin by assigning two or three sentences, radically increasing the amount to be read as the group rotates. In the initial stages of Peer Control, the teacher is part of the group, one of the Correctors. The teacher models for the group, pointing out the types of errors for which they should watch. Whenever the teacher stops the Reader, he asks the group to identify the error. If the group cannot recognize the error, the teacher gives them the name of the error and asks them to tell him, in their own words, what the error was. The teacher then asks the group for the correct response. If the group does not know the correct answer, the teacher then shows them how to find it. For example, if the error is a mispronunciation (dialect pronunciation, such as "doe" for "door" is acceptable), the teacher gives the group a short lesson in word attack skills and demonstrates how to use the dictionary for such purposes.

The teacher, as a member of the group, helps the group to first recognize and correct simple errors, then gradually more complex ones. The types of errors the teacher alerts the group to from his position as one of the Correctors are not limited to oral reading skills per se. The teacher may stop the Reader and ask her to summarize what she has read. If the Reader cannot give a summary statement, it is considered a comprehension error. The teacher explains to the group that the Reader must first understand what she is reading. Comprehension is stressed in the group.

The teacher gradually turns control of the group process over to the students and eventually leaves the group. At this point, the teacher re-enters the group only when the Correctors have spotted an error but do not know the correct response. The teacher also enters the group when she hears the group consistently overlooking certain errors or when she wishes to inject additional errors for the group to spot.

Relationship to How Children Learn in Their Natural Environment

The Peer Control Procedure grew out of observations of how Black non-mainstream children learn in their natural environment. The natural learning mode from which Peer Control was adapted is called "playing the dozens." Playing the dozens, also called "sounding" and "woofing," is a game of ritualistic verbal insults engaged in by small groups for entertainment and for sharpening and validating one's verbal skills. It is a contest of spontaneous verbal facility performed in front of a small audience.

Although playing the dozens is usually viewed from a pathological perspective by social scientists, the author views it as a cultural convention with educational implications—a group mechanism which gives practice, feedback, reinforcement and recognition to the individual's verbal skills through competition. The following excerpt was taken from an actual tape of Black non-mainstream students engaged in a Peer Control exercise:

Reader: So, Jim went down the hall to John Fox's apartment. He knew that John Fox was a good reader. He told John Fox that he had brought a me-al box...

Corrector: Hold tight, stop! You just made one of them mistakes that they call mispronunciation. Check it, the word was metal, and you said he had brought a me-al box. You got that, METAL, like iron, baby. Now, back it up and try one more time.

Reader: So, Jim went down the hall to John Fox's apartment. He knew that John Fox was a good reader. He told John Fox that he bought a...

Corrector: Stop it right there, my man. And let's get this to-
             gether. You done made a mistake called omission.
             That's when you skip over a word that you wasn't
             'pose to skip over. You understand what I'm trying
             to say? You read, "He told John Fox he brought,"
             instead of "He told John Fox he had brought." You
             left out "had" and that ain't too cool. So let's back it
             up again.

Reader: So, Jim went down the hall to John Fox's apartment.
             He knew that John Fox was a good reader. He told
             John Fox that he had bought a metal box and a
             combination lock so he could protect his valuable
             possessions.

Corrector: Alright! Go ahead, with your bad self. You finally
             got it together.

Reader: Yeah, and I hope you be next. 'Cause I'm gon keep
             you reading for days.

The Peer Control Procedure also draws heavily on the "call-and-response" oral tradition of the Black community, which is seen in the call-and-response behavior of the Black church where the audience becomes an active participant with the speaker.

In the typical classroom, one can observe interactions similar to playing the dozens. The teacher can, and often does (intentionally or unintentionally) "sound on the student" i.e., give negative comments. But the student cannot retort within the rules of the classroom for there is an unequal power distribution between the student and the teacher. Although in playing the dozens, the participants begin equal in terms of power, the route to greater power is through greater verbal competence. Thus, the one who displays the greatest verbal competence becomes the high status-

power person and receives the lion's share of the positive reinforcement.

Past observations (Simpkins, 1973; Houghton Mifflin, 1975)
have shown that the Peer Control Procedure is autotelic. The term
"autotelic" describes the quality of an instructional sequence which
becomes an end in itself, so that perceiving the sequence is intrinsically reinforcing. Students tend to engage in Peer Control for its
own sake, rather than for extrinsic rewards or punishments. Teachers have reported that often students do not want to disengage
from their Peer Control groups when the bell rings to end the
class.

The Peer Control Procedure approximates the mechanics of
expansive program learning systems. Knowledge of the correctness or incorrectness of the student's responses to the reading
materials is supplied in close temporal relation to the responses by
a built-in feedback system. An incorrect response is identified and
immediately followed by a stimulus event which serves to inform
the Reader of the nature of the correct response. The Reader is
then recycled back to an earlier successful stage. Reinforcement is
contingent upon the Reader's response in a manner which leads to
the shaping of skillful reading behavior.

6

Guidelines for Developing Instructional Materials

The development of Cross-Cultural instructional materials encompasses two components: (a) the development of instructional materials which reflect Black language and culture, and (b) the development of instructional materials which reflect mainstream language and culture. The development of instructional materials which reflect mainstream language and culture does not pose a problem for educators. An abundance of books and other forms of literature exist on the subject. There are many programs which can be used as models. In addition, there is a clearly defined prescription formula for using the standard mainstream dialect, and clearly delineated developmental norms based on extensive research. But when it comes to the development of instructional materials which reflect Black language and culture, a completely different situation exists. There is a poverty of literature. There are few, if any, programs that can be used as models. There is no clearly defined prescriptive formula for using African American Language and no developmental norms based on research.

Due to the availability of information on the development of mainstream instructional materials and the conspicuous lack of information on African American Language instructional materials, the focus of this chapter is on the development of Black non-mainstream instructional materials. In developing instructional materials for Black non-mainstream students, one of the most important variables, and the most distinguishing features, is the language used in the materials. Language is sometimes conceptualized by educators as a neutral terrain, devoid of any attachment to a culture, where one might justifiably correct students for using "substandard English" without implications of cultural ethnocentrism or racism. Such notions are at best a convenient naivete. Concepts such as "standard English" and "substandard English," when applied to African American Language, are, from a linguistic perspective, clearly a product of cultural ethnocentrism.

Black children learn and speak the language of those persons who are closest and most meaningful to them. When educators conceptualize the language that Black children bring to the schools as "substandard" or "deficient" rather than different, they are guilty of cultural ethnocentrism. When educators correct the children, verbally or with nonverbal signals, for using "substandard English" rather than telling the children that they wish to teach them a different dialect of the language, they are guilty of cultural aggression against Black culture, the children, the parents of the children, and the larger Black community which speaks African American Language. One cannot disparage the language of a group of people without disparaging the culture of that group. Language is the primary conveyor of culture; and in an oral culture, language and culture are inextricably bound together.

If one rejects the cultural deprivation hypothesis that Black children are deprived of a suitable language and culture, then one is led to place a great deal of importance on the sociocultural context in which the children learn and use their language. The

African American Language in this country stems from an oral tradition. Hence, the dialect is learned by Black children solely from the sociocultural context or the environment in which it is used.

Linguists have recently devoted a great deal of attention to the study of African American Language. They have delineated certain phonological, syntactical, and lexical features closely associated with African American Language speakers. The work of these linguists constitutes a giant step forward in the scientific study of African American Language. They have provided accurate and reliable information about the language of the vast majority of Black people to combat the myths, stereotypes, and falsehoods which have historically been accepted by educators and the general public in this country.

But, one must be cognizant of the fact that research on African American Language is not a closed book. A great deal of information is simply not available. For example, little is known about the rules which control the mixing of dialect features and Standard English. There is no prescriptive formula for speaking African American Language, and perhaps more important to the developer of instructional materials, there is no prescriptive formula for writing in African American Language: nor are there developmental norms or stages.

Developers of instructional materials have attempted to use the features discovered by linguists to be closely associated with dialect speakers as a system of rules, as a prescriptive formula for translating from Standard English to African American Language. The end product of this procedure is usually reading materials that are stilted, lifeless, colorless, unnatural and stereotypic. The materials, often unintentionally miss the beauty, richness, humor and poetry of African American Language and Black culture. The materials often portray the speakers as dull or stupid.

In any language or dialect of a language there are varying degrees of ability among speakers. There are those speakers who are articulate and those who are inarticulate; there are speakers who possess little verbal facility, and those who have exceptional verbal facility. In the case of Standard English, a great deal of research has been devoted to the assessment of verbal ability and language development norms. Out of this research, numerous instruments for measuring verbal ability have been developed. Well defined norms have been established.

In the case of African American Language there are no standardized instruments for assessing verbal ability or language developmental stages. Educators generally assess Black children's language ability by using norms and instruments developed for mainstream English speakers. They overlook the fact that verbal ability and language developmental norms can be meaningfully ascertained only in the context of the children's dialect and culture. Norms which characterize one dialect and culture should not be automatically applied to other dialects of that language that represents a different culture.

Certain kinds of differences among cultural groups interfere with the assessment of student's language ability. For example, it would be foolish to assess White mainstream student's ability to play the dozens as a measure of language ability. For this population, the ability to play the dozens is not an important cultural convention and for the most part, such students would score low on such an assessment device.

Faced with a lack of instruments and norms based on research in the Black community, the developer of instructional materials in African American Language must turn to the cultural context in which the dialect is used for the norms and standards of excellence. The developer must be knowledgeable of those individuals in the Black non-mainstream community who are considered by the community to be highly proficient verbally; those "Brothers and Sisters" who can really "get down with the language." The developer must know the cultural conventions, oral tradition, and range of variability of the language. It is the lack of a functional conceptualization of excellence and variability of African American Language based on norms that can be observed in the Black community, which prevents developers from designing acceptable instructional materials. It is this lack that causes the Black community to be highly critical of the pedagogical use of African American Language.

Although one can find in the literature numerous accounts of Black people's rejecting the pedagogical use of African American Language, my experiences with the Black community have been quite the opposite. If the instructional materials portray authentic (not stereotypical) vernacular, are true to Black non-mainstream culture, empathic to Black students and Black culture, and are of literary and educational value, the Black community readily embraces them.

> Most efforts to use African American Language in reading materials fail to take into account Black people's sensitivity to its pejorative uses. Materials that were psychological carbons of stereotypical literature, inherently offensive to Black people, were dated and doomed from the moment of their publication. Thus, it was the manner of realizing the dialect for literary purposes which created the offense, not the idea of using the dialect per se (Holt, 1974).

A basic premise of the Cross-Cultural Approach pertaining to the development of instructional reading materials can now be stated: "**The developer of instructional materials and the intended consumer of those materials must share a common**

cultural and linguistic background (Simpkins, 1973)." All too often the literature on Black culture and language is distorted, written from a mainstream culturally ethnocentric perspective. What one frequently finds in the literature is Black culture viewed through the eyes of culturally ethnocentric mainstream social scientists.

A prerequisite for the development of cross-cultural instructional materials in AAVE is that the developer know the language and culture of Black people from a phenomenological perspective. The developer must learn African American Language from an experiential frame of reference in cultural context rather than solely from instruction and the literature.

This should not be interpreted to mean that only Blacks can develop instructional materials for Black non-mainstream children. If the developer does not have an experiential perspective, then the developer should enlist the aid of someone who is familiar with the language and culture of Black people. This person should not be utilized as an informant, but as an integral part of the project, with shared decision-making power over instructional context and style.

Diversity of Subject Matter

A common misconception is that the developers of instructional reading materials in African American Language are limited in the content area. Although it is of critical importance that instructional materials honestly reflect Black culture, this requirement in no way imposes limits on the content area. Developers are often tempted to write exclusively about those things that are considered to uniquely characterize Black culture and the Black community. All too often this practice leads the developer to write exclusively about the deprivation, violence, or anger of the community.

The critical variables in selecting subject matter for African American Language instructional materials are not the unique experiences, or events, but the different cultural expressions of shared human experiences or events. Upon close examination, one will discover that there are very few experiences of people in the Black community, from conception to death, that are different or unique. The experiences become differently or uniquely expressed as a function of the cultural context in which they occurred. For example, children growing up in the Black community share many of the same experiences as children growing up in the mainstream community. They experience a father, a mother, love, happiness, tears, separation, and neglect. Contrary to the notions of "cultural" and "sensory deprivations," the experiences of Black people are by no means limited. Their experiences are differentiated by cultural, historical, economic and personal considerations.

The developers' only limit in developing instructional materials which reflect Black culture is their knowledge of Black culture, language and students—and their own creativity. Three examples of stories which illustrate the diversity of experiences and themes in the Black cultural context, around which reading instructional materials can be developed are included. It is important for the reader to note that the experiences and themes occur in both Black and mainstream culture.

Elaborating the Benefits of Literacy Through Reading Material

A frequent complaint of teachers working with Black non-mainstream students is that nothing they do seems to motivate the students to want to learn to read better. The students are just not interested in reading. Many teachers suggest that the problem is in the homes. The students do not see the need for reading or reading improvement because literacy is not valued in the homes or in the students' immediate environment. The students seldom see any books or reading materials around their homes and therefore they have no models with which to relate. In addition, teachers are quick to point out that the values of the students' peer group are antipathetic and often hostile toward literacy.

At a workshop I was conducting, a teacher told me that she had become totally frustrated trying to instill an appreciation for reading and general literacy in her Black non-mainstream students. She said that she had tried everything possible, but to no avail. She had tried exposing her students to the great literary works of western civilization. They were bored. She invited Black professionals who were highly literate to talk to the students about the need for reading and general literacy in their work. The students were unimpressed. She talked about and read to them the works of famous Black authors like James Baldwin and William Dubois. The students were inattentive. She took the class on a field trip to a Black newspaper. Not one expressed any interest in journalism.

This teacher was different in that she was more energetic than most teachers. But the problem she related is one shared by the vast majority of teachers working with Black non-mainstream students. The frustration she felt is shared by a great many teachers.

As simplistic as it may seem, the problem—lack of interest in reading and general literacy—is caused in part by the failure of the schools to tell the students why they should learn to read in a manner that is meaningful to them in their everyday life. They have told them repeatedly that it is important for them to learn to read well in order for them to obtain employment "sitting behind a desk." It is important to learn to read well so that they can become a doctor, or a lawyer, or an engineer. In essence, they have told them that it is important to learn to read well so that they can benefit in the future in a different setting.

Seldom are the benefits of reading and general literacy explained to the students in their immediate natural environment. That is not to say that long-term goals are not important, or that there is something wrong with pointing out the benefits of reading and literacy as they relate to prestigious professions. But what needs to be pointed out is a "happy mixture" of long-term and immediate benefits. This is based on the realization that it is increasingly difficult for the learner to strive for long-term goals or benefits when the learner sees few immediate or short-term benefits.

It is of critical importance that the benefits of reading and general literacy and the disadvantages of illiteracy are elaborated to the learners in a manner which relates to their immediate natural environment and life style. Reading instructional materials can and should be written to accomplish this goal. To accomplish this task, the developers of reading instructional materials must take experiences, information, values, attitudes and themes concerning the advantages and disadvantages of general literacy and translate them into the learners' familiar cultural context.

The general instructional principle is: **The developers of instructional reading materials must hold constant the general concepts relating to the advantages or disadvantages of literacy they wish to convey to the learners, while allowing the content and cultural context of the instructional materials to vary in order to match the immediate natural environment and language of the consumers.** Two examples of stories which serve to illustrate this principle can be found in this book.

Black Folklore

Black folklore is an excellent source of content material reflecting Black culture. Black folklore can be considered as Black oral history passed down from generation to generation. Black folklore is a rich, imaginative, colorful source of Black oral literature, culture and heritage. Unfortunately, most libraries and schools have ignored this body of oral literature and concentrated on folklore which reflects the European heritage. A vast body of folklore known as oral epic poetry, or "toasts" has been almost completely ignored. In recent years with the upsurge of interest in African American Language this body of folklore has been "discovered" by researchers.

Oral epic poetry is, perhaps, one of the best sources of content material for instructional reading material reflecting Black culture. This body of folklore is an outgrowth of African folklore's coming into contact with the New World, the experience of slavery and the aftermath of slavery—the urbanization of Blacks. It belongs to the Black person in the streets. With the exception of those narratives which describe certain specific historical events, it is difficult to date. The oral epic poetry narratives are generally regarded by Black people as part of the developmental exposure of non-mainstream Blacks—part of the Black culture. They appear to have no geographical focal point. They are as well known in the South as in the North, in the East as in the West. At one time almost all Black people who had grown up in inner-city settings were acquainted with this body of folklore. A story based on Black folklore which serves to illustrate the vast potential of this body of oral literature as a source of content materials for reading instructional materials can be found later in this book.

Skill-Related Materials

Traditionally, as well as currently, most reading programs and approaches teach reading skills by having the students engage in mass practice at problem solving through skills exercises. Problems are given and the students' task is to find the answers. It is assumed that by finding the answers to items in an exercise, the students will gain proficiency in a particular skill related to reading. Emphasis is placed on mass problem solving rather than on instructing the students how to find the answer. Often the students are not told how to find the answer: they are simply given the correct answer.

In the Cross-Cultural Approach, the emphasis is placed instead on understanding the concept underlying the particular skill. In explaining concepts, the students are given (a) a statement of purpose; (b) an explanation of the concepts underlying the skill, designed to show them how to work the skill; and (c) a series of examples on how to apply the skill.

The Cross-Cultural Approach makes the assumption that the best way for Black students to understand skill-related concepts is to put the concepts in the students' familiar language and cultural context. This approach assumes that once the students understand the concepts in their familiar dialect and cultural context, they can generalize the concepts to mainstream English, and then to their everyday school reading activities. It assumes that the best way to teach reading-related skills is to start the students with the familiar, in terms of their language and culture, and take them in a series of steps to the less familiar.

Some of the basic assumptions for using the students' familiar cultural context in the skill-related materials are as follows:

a) the cultural context represents ways of thinking and doing things which are normal to a culture;

b) the cultural context influences the ways in which students engage in such cognitive activities as recall, rule setting, and task orientation;

c) by starting with the familiar cultural context, the added cognitive operation-translation, which Black students must often perform in order to process the concepts, is eliminated;
   and

d) the familiar cultural context supplies intrinsic reinforcement,
   thus serving as a greater success facilitator than the less
   familiar.

7

The Genesis of the Bridge Reading Program

First Attempts in Los Angeles

After the death of Martin Luther King, Jr., Technomics Research and Analysis Corporation, a Los Angeles based scientific company, undertook at its personal expense, the task of attacking the problem of widespread reading failure among non-white youths in urban ghettos. I was engaged by Technomics as a special consultant on the project.

Burton R. Wolin, Ph.D., Vice President of Research at Technomics, and I designed a reading and writing instructional package tailored to the language and experience of Black urban ghetto youths of high school age "who had never experienced the benefits of reading." The design of the instructional package was based on available knowledge culled from research on reading, learning theory, African American Language (AAL) and untested ideas of Dr. Wolin and myself.

Reading materials were designed to start the students in their familiar African American Language and take them to Standard English. Prior to the writing of the materials, a dialect survey was conducted in the Los Angeles area. The purpose of the survey was to update my familiarity with the verbal behavior and interest of the target population, Black ghetto youths (male and female) of junior and senior high school age. Speech samples were collected in the various inner-city areas of Los Angeles—at Teen Posts, settlement houses, playgrounds and other locations where Black inner-city youths congregated.

In addition, I spent a number of weeks interacting with youths, watching the target population characteristics. I visited a variety of settings: on basketball courts, in pool halls, at parties and, on a number of occasions, sitting on the grass at neighborhood parks drinking wine with dropouts. When engaged in these activities I dressed, walked and spoke in the manner of the target population. Since I am a native speaker of African American Language, I was able to relate quite successfully to the youths on both a verbal and cultural level.

The materials developed in the Los Angeles area were in the form of short stories written in three versions: (a) Offensive Vernacular (OV); (b) Neutral Vernacular (NV); and (c) Standard English (SE). Each version of the story consisted of approximately three pages. No formula was followed in writing the stories; i.e., they were not translated from Standard English or composed via a set of linguistic rules. The stories were written by me to reflect the experiential frame of reference of members of the target population in terms of objects and events in their environment. Most of the sets of stories carried a hidden theme of "why learn to read," presented in a manner congruent with the value system of the youth. For example, "learn to read because it can keep you from losing your cool" was a hidden theme of one of the stories.

The stories were written in the following sequence: First a story line was sketched in dialect. This was then expanded into a rough draft of four or five pages, drawing freely on Offensive Vernacular words, terms, and phrases. The story was then rewritten, edited, and polished until the writer was satisfied with the outcome. Next, a second, Neutral Vernacular (NV) version was developed. The story was stripped of all Offensive Vernacular and appropriate euphemisms in African American Language substituted. For example, "motherfucker" was changed to "sucker" and "shit" changed to "stuff." The substitutions were analogous to the changes in dialect terminology that Black youth often make when moving from peer setting to a family or school setting. After completion of the Offensive Vernacular version and the Neutral Vernacular version, the story was then translated into Standard English see Neutral Vernacular and Standard English versions below.

NV Version

Bill Smith, an old Brother from the South, had gotten some bread from an accident twenty years ago. With the dough he got himself an apartment building. The old Brother was out in front of his building watering his lawn. This fine little Sister, named Pat, came up an asks the old Brother if she could see the pad for rent. The Sister had dug on a "for rent" sign stuck in the lawn.

The old Brother say, "No, Sister, 'cause ain't nobody here."

The Sister rapped back, "You're here, honey. Why can't you show me the pad?"

"'Cause I ain't the manager."

The Sister asked, "Where can I find the dude? And who is you, baby?"

"I'm the owner, but I ain't the manager."

SE Version

Bill Smith was in front of his apartment watering his lawn. A prospective tenant, Pat Jones, came up to inquire about a vacancy. Bill Smith said that he couldn't help Pat Jones. He said that she would have to come back the next day if she wished to see the apartment. Pat asked where and when she could contact the owner.

Bill Smith informed her that he was the owner. This surprised Pat. She could not understand why she couldn't see the apartment. She asked, "Why can't I see the apartment now?"

Bill Smith told her that the manager would have to show her the apartment and that he wasn't around at the present time.

The instructional package was evaluated under the auspices of California State College at Los Angeles with Neighborhood Youth Corps enrollees as subjects. The evaluation was conducted at my expense, in collaboration with Technomics, because of a lack of funds at Technomics.

The results of the initial evaluation seemed to indicate that certain sections of the materials and procedures were effective in teaching Black inner-city students to improve their reading. The results also indicated a need for extended research and development.

Boston Revisions and Evaluations

Based on findings from the initial evaluation, additional knowledge from current research in reading, African American Language, and learning theory, the reading package was rewritten in the Boston area. Because of the unfavorable reactions received from the educational community (Black and White), the Offensive Vernacular version was eliminated from the package.

The new reading package consisted of short stories written in three versions: Street Vernacular (SV); Written Vernacular (WV); and Standard English (SE). The Street Vernacular version was devoid of all Offensive Vernacular. The SV version was written as close to street spoken conversation as possible and was generally a page or two longer than the other versions. The Written Vernacular version of the story had a tighter structure than the SV version in terms of syntax and paragraph structure. It was closer to Standard English than the Street Vernacular version, but was essentially written in African American Language. The Standard English version remained the same as the Los Angeles version.

The reading materials were divided into four sections. The first section contained five stories in three versions. These stories contained the hidden theme, "why learn to read." The second section contained four stories in two versions (Street Vernacular and Written Vernacular). The third section contained two stories in Street Vernacular. The last section contained two stories in Standard English.

Several of the stories used in the package were based on a body of Black folklore known as oral epic poetry or "toasts." This body of folklore was an outgrowth of African folklore coming into contact with the New World, the experience of slavery, the aftermath of slavery, and the urbanization of Black people.

Prior to writing new materials and modifying existing materials in the Boston area, I spent several months interacting with youths of the target population in the Roxbury and South End areas of Boston. This was accomplished in a manner similar to the Los Angeles survey, with similar results.

After the materials were modified and new materials developed, three groups of fifteen Black ghetto youngsters were selected from Roxbury, Mattapan, and the South End. The criteria used for selection were that they be Black, poor, between the ages of twelve and eighteen and have lived in Boston for at least half their lives.

The youths were given a tape recording of four stories in African American Language, recorded by a fluent speaker of the dialect from Los Angeles who had recently moved to Boston to attend graduate school. Two of the stories were developed in Los Angeles and two were developed in Boston. After listening to the stories, the youths were asked three questions:

1. Who do you think wrote the stories and where do you think the writer lives?
2. Where do you think the characters the writer was writing about are from?
3. Do the characters in the story talk like you, your friends or family?

The objective of these procedures was to determine if the materials developed in Los Angeles and the new materials were compatible with the dialect of Boston youths and to assess whether regional differences were substantial enough to render the material inappropriate for the Boston area. Based on responses to the questions, it was decided that regional differences were not substantial enough to justify conducting a formal dialect survey or excluding the reading material developed in Los Angeles.

The new reading program was developed and evaluated under the auspices of the Research Institute for Educational Problems in Cambridge, Massachusetts. An evaluation of the package was conducted in the Roxbury area of Boston at a local boys' club. The results of the evaluation suggested that the reading package was effective in teaching Black inner-city youths to quickly improve their reading, but also indicated a need for further research and development.

The National Edition

In 1973, Houghton Mifflin Publishing Company formed an Urban Programs Department within their Educational Division. The charge of Urban Programs was to publish innovative educational programs aimed at minority communities. I was approached by the Director of the Urban Programs Department and told that the reading program under study was highly recommended by Black educators and researchers in various parts of the country. An appointment was arranged between the author and the Director to review the reading program and to discuss the possibilities of Houghton Mifflin's publishing the program.

I agreed to develop a comprehensive reading program. The agreement was contingent upon Houghton Mifflin's allowing me to choose my writing team and committing the company's resources to a field test of the program in the public schools. In addition, I insisted that the publishing company agree not to market the program unless both I and the publishing company agreed that the field test data indicated the program was an effective tool for teaching Black inner-city students to improve their reading.

The national edition of the reading program, which came to be known as *Bridge: A Cross-Cultural Reading Program*, funded under the auspices of Houghton Mifflin, was field tested in various parts of the country in February of 1975. The results were extremely promising. Both I and the publishing company agreed that the data clearly indicated that the program was effective (see chapter 10). Based on the data from the field test, a final edition of the program was prepared.

In December, 1976, one month prior to the release of *Bridge: A Cross Cultural Reading Program* by Houghton Mifflin Publishing Company an article on the program's field test results appeared in *Newsweek* magazine (see Appendix 1). The article described the reading program and presented data from its highly impressive field test.

The article ignited a firestorm of controversy centered around the pedagogical use of African American Language. On television and radio talk shows, in editorials and other public forums an endless parade of speakers voiced their negative opinions on the use of AAL in the classroom. While there was no lack of commentary from African Americans, it was noted that the respondents were all from the middle class.

The publishers and authors were accused of being co-conspirators in a plot to lock Black students into ghetto English, to elevate the status of African American Language to that of Standard English and to water down the public schools curriculum. The stigma and myths associated with African American Language roared throughout the country.

Black and White professionals who knew little about language and even less about inner-city children (to paraphrase Labov) spouted an unremitting stream of platitudes on the full consequences of using African American Language in the schools. They conceptualized AAL as a form of standard used by gang members, drug addicts, the poor and ignorant, and those youths who had failed to master or even quite comprehend Standard English. The situation in 1976-77 began to parallel what Noam Chomsky describes as the "manufacturing of consent," the media manipulation of information to present or highlight certain views of an issue and play down or even exclude contradictory opinions.

I spoke extensively with Black non-mainstream parents, teachers, and community leaders throughout the country and, without exception, I found them highly supportive of the Bridge Project. Once they understood what the reading program consisted of, its philosophy, theory, and goals, they endorsed the program.

A good example of this community acceptance was the Roxbury community in Boston. As a result of the many research projects conducted in the Black non-mainstream community by Harvard and other schools in the area, the community had formed the Community Research Review Committee (CRRC). After rejecting a research project by Harvard psychologist Jerome Kagan, the CRRC enthusiastically endorsed my request to conduct research and development on the Bridge Reading Program.

I did not experience any resistance to the reading program or the use of AAL at the community level. The opposition came from outside the Black non-mainstream community. It came from professionals whose children were doing well in school and did not attend inner-city schools or public schools in general. It was orchestrated by the media and given validation by Black middle class professionals. In the end, the negative media coverage and negative statements by government and education officials, combined with the response of the Black middle class, prevented the *Bridge Program* from being used in schools.

• • •

Why does the mere mention of including African American Language in an educational program cause people to rage, rant, ridicule, and overreact? It has a great deal to do with the fact that AAL is associated with Black people historically (The White Man's Burden). In America it is acceptable for an individual to maintain an ethnic identity and dialect such as Polish, Jewish, German, or Irish without being considered crude or of low intelligence. It is acceptable for a Congressman or Senator to speak in a heavy White Southern rural dialect without his intelligence or his morality being questioned. He is often even considered to be witty and colorful. But in this country, having a Black identity, or speaking in a way that identifies one as being Black, tends to automatically elicit a negative response pattern.

After reviewing the media coverage on "The Ebonics Issue", Wayne O'Neil (2000) observed that criticism of Black language (AAL) was the last bastion where one could freely espouse racist attitudes and comments without fear of public recrimination.

Patricia Young (2000), while analyzing the Bridge Reading Program and other historically significant instructional materials and systems designed by Blacks for Blacks, concluded that AAL is misunderstood by the White population:

> "The misunderstanding of Black English is analogous to the misunderstanding of Black people as a race. Black English has been viewed in deficit terms because of its association with Black people."

8

The Bridge
Reading Program

The Bridge Reading Program is an excellent example of the type of research and development which comes from a 'difference model' perspective. It represents a creative synthesis of the research from theorists cited in this book who viewed the Black non-mainstream child as uniquely different in his language and culture. The works of William Labov can be singled out as having the most profound influence on me. His research helped me to view the Black non-mainstream child as a unique entity and focus on his strengths rather than his weaknesses.

The Bridge Reading Program was written by an interdisciplinary team of authors composed of a psychologist, a linguist and a reading specialist. The program took into consideration that Black non-mainstream children know more about reading and Standard English then they are able to display on tests. The problem is that there are gaps in their learning which prevent them from putting it all together.

Black non-mainstream children are immersed in Standard English. They do not spend as many hours as they do, looking at television and movies, without understanding a great deal about Standard English. Often, they have good receptive abilities but have not quite acquired productive abilities. They do not know where AAL stops and where SE begins. They find it difficult to perform the fine discriminations that are necessary to code switch. While they know a great deal about Standard English, the gaps in their learning prevent them from seeing it as a unified whole. The Bridge Reading Program was designed to fill these gaps.

The overriding goal of the reading program was to break the vicious cycle of the cumulative deficit these students experience. Once this cycle is broken, the student, many for the first time in their academic careers, experience the joy of learning and the reinforcement which comes from being successful in school.

Description of Materials

The Bridge Reading Program is organized into five sections. Each section has its own reading booklet and its own study book containing questions, exercises and Peer Control stories. There is also a set of recordings on four cassettes. For the Teacher there is an annotated Teacher's Edition of each study book and a comprehensive Teacher's Guide to the entire program.

The stories are coded to indicate the dialect used, African American Language (AAL) Transition (T) and Standard English (SE).

1) African American Language (AAL)
   The term African American Language, as used in this program, refers to the speech commonly heard in many Black communities. The African American Language stories use the sentence patterns, vocabulary and figures of speech indigenous to speakers of this vernacular. The content of these stories reflects aspects of Black culture.

2) Transition (T)

The Transition stories use a combination of African American Language and Standard English. Transition versions of the stories are an important step in moving students from reading in African American Language to reading in Standard English.

3) Standard English (SE)

The Standard English stories use the customary dialect used in educational materials. The ultimate success of Bridge is dependent on the students' success in reading Standard English.

Any story presented in more than one dialect version—African American Language, Transition and/or Standard English—is not presented as a literal, word-for-word translation. The basic plot remains unchanged from version to version, but names of characters and certain details and events may differ. Students therefore will not be able to rely on their memory of an earlier version of a story to do the Study Book exercises for the later version.

The five reading booklets contain 22 stories arranged according to the associative bridging sequence are briefly described below. To get a feel for the African American Language several are reprinted in whole or in part, some in their transition form.

Booklet One

There are four stories in Booklet One, written in AAL. *Shine*, the story most popular with the students, and *Stagolee* have their origins in Black folklore. The stories, *The Organizer* and *The Ghost* occur in what was then a contemporary inner-city setting.

In the story *Shine*, the main character is a Black man, a stoker on the ill-fated Titanic. As stoker, it is his job to shovel coal into the ship's furnace. He repeatedly warns the captain that the ship is sinking. The Captain refuses to listen and the ship sinks. As Shine jumps off the ship and saves himself, various people on the ship implore him to save them. A sample story in African American Language:

Shine: A Story in African American Language

This story come from Black folklore, you understand. Black folklore is stories that Black folk have told and sung for a whole lot of years. This here story is all about Shine, a strong Black man! Maybe you heard other stories about Shine. Now come here and check out mine.

You ever hear of the Titanic? Yeah, that's right. It was one of them big ships. The kind they call a ocean liner. Now this here ship was the biggest and the baddest ship ever to sail the sea. You understand? It was suppose to be unsinkable. Wind, storm, iceberg – nothing could get next to it. It was a superbad ship, the meanest on the water. It could move like four Bloods in tennis shoes. It was out of sight!

But you know what? The very first time this here ship put out to sea, it got sunk. Can you get ready for that? On its first trip, this here bad, superbad ship got sunk. Now ain't that something.

Well anyway, this here bad, superbad ship went under. Word was, there was a very few survivors. Just about everybody got drown. But quiet as it's kept, they say that one dude who got away was a Blood. Yeah, can you get ready for that? He was a big, Black, strong Brother by the name of Shine.

Shine was a stoker on the Titanic. The Brother, he shovel coal into the ship furnace to make the engines go. Now dig. Check what went down on the day the Titanic sunk. Shine kept on going up to the captain of the ship. He kept on telling the captain that the ship was leaking.

Shine run on up to the captain and say, "Captain, Captain, I was down in the hole looking for something to eat. And you know what? The water rose above my feet."

The captain say, "Shine, Shine, boy, have no doubt. We got ninety-nine pumps to pump the water out. Now boy, get back down in the hole and start shoveling some more coal."

Shine went on back down the hole. He start to shoveling coal, singing, "Lord, Lord, please have mercy on my soul." As Shine was singing, *Lord, Lord, Please*, the water rose above his knees.

Shine split back up on deck and say, "Captain, Captain I was down in the hole. I was shoveling coal and singing *Lord, Lord, Please* and you know what? The water, it rose above my knees."

The captain told Shine that all was cool. He say, "Shine, Shine, I done told you to have no doubt. Boy, we got ninety-nine pumps to pump the water out. Now get on back in the hole and just keep shoveling coal."

Shine went back down in the hole. He kept on shoveling coal. He stop to wipe the sweat off is face. That's when the water rose above his waist.

Shine run back up on deck. He say, "Captain, Captain, I was down in the hole just shoveling coals and when I stop to wipe the sweat off my face, the water, it rose above my waist!"

The captain say, "Shine, Shine, boy, now how many time do I have to tell you to have no doubt? If I done told you once, I don told you a hundred times. We got ninety-nine pumps to pump the water out. Now boy, don't you trust your captain? I don't want to see you on deck again, You hear?"

Shine went on back down in the hole. He kept on shoveling coal. He start to eat a piece of bread. That's when the water rose above the Brother's head.

Shine split back up on deck. "Captain, Captain, you speak well, and you words, they sound true. But this time, Captain, your words they won't do. This here ship is sinking! Little fishes, big fishes, whales and sharks too, get out of my way, 'cause I'm coming through."

Shine yanked off his clothes in a flash. He jumped on in the water and started to splash.

The captain saw the water rise out of the hole and he start thinking, "That boy is right, this here ship is sinking." He call out to Shine, "Shine, Mr. Shine, please save me! I'll make you master of the sea!"

Shine say, "Master on land, master on sea, if you want to live, Captain, you better jump in here and swim like me."

The captain's wife ran out on deck in her nightgown, with her fine, fine self. She call out to Shine, "Shine, Shine please save poor me! I'll give you more loving than you ever did see."

Shine say, "Loving ain't nothing but hugging and squeezing. Sometime it be tiring. Sometime it be pleasing. I can swim, but I ain't no fish. I like loving, but not like this."

An old fat banker come up on deck carrying his money bags. He called out to Shine, "Shine, Shine, please save me! I'll make you richer than any man could be."

Shine say, "Money's good on land, but it's weight in the sea. If you want to live, fatty, you better jump in here and swim like me."

Shine took one stroke and shot on off through the water like a motorboat. He met up with this here shark. The shark say, "Shine, Shine, you swim so fine. But if you miss one stroke, your butt is mine."

Shine say, "I swims the ocean, I swims the sea. There just ain't no shark that can outswim me." Shine outswimmed the shark.

After a while, Shine met up with this here whale. The whale say, "I'm king of the ocean. I'm king of the sea."

Shine say, "You may be king of the ocean. And you just may be king of the sea, but you got to be about a swimming sucker to outswim me." Shine outswimmed the whale.

Now dig this. When the news reach land that the Great Titanic had sunk, Shine was down on the corner, half-way drunk.

• • •

The story *Stagolee*, like *Shine*, is a classic in Black folklore. Stagolee was the biggest , baddest, meanest, dirtiest and toughest of all the lead men. He was a man who lived his life 'his way.'

The story, *The Organizer* examines a group of inner-city friends and their entrepreneurial leader who they all admire. They discover that their leader cannot read. This story carries the theme 'why learn to read?' and illustrates the social stigma of not being able to read.

The story *The Ghost* is a humorous tale about Willie, a hard-headed kid who would not listen to anyone. In the story, Willie gets himself expelled from school and loses his job because of a negative attitude. He then decides to go into the armed services against his parents' wishes. When his parents receive word that Willie is killed in action, they pray every night to see their deceased son one more time. The neighbors, who live above the parents, long for an end to the nightly ritual of loud praying and movements. So the neighbors put on a white sheet and pretend to be Willie.

Booklet Two

There are two stories presented in Booklet Two: *Old, But Not Defenseless* and *What I Got to be Proud Of*. Both stories are written in African American Language and Transition versions.

Old, But Not Defenseless is an inner-city version of Little Red Riding Hood. Geraldine, the main character of the AAL version goes through the park to get to her grandmother's house with a gift of sweet bread. She encounters a friendly man who offers to walk her to her grandmothers. Geraldine, remembering her mothers warning against strangers, refuses his offer. At grandmother's house, the grandmother tells Geraldine how to defend herself.

In the Transition version of *Old, But Not Defenseless*, Geraldine carries a bottle of homemade wine to her grandmother. She is dressed in a dashiki. She is followed to her grandmother's house by a man posing as an insurance salesman, who wants grandmother's home made wine.

Old, But Not Defenseless: A Story in African American Language

"Geraldine, come her girl. I want you to take this hot sweet bread over to Big Mama's house. Carry the bag right side up. Or else you mess up the icing. Get it there while it warm. Don't you be playing around. You hear?" Geraldine's mama say.

"Yes, Mama. I'm gone!" Say Geraldine. She carry the cake upright. She didn't want to mess up the icing or nothing.

It was the first day of summer and it was hot! It was even hotter holding that hot cake! It was so hot that Geraldine took this short cut through the park. Geraldine knew her folks didn't like her to be going through no park. She could hear Mama talking now. "Those men in that park, they like wild bears. You can't trust them. You can't turn your back on them. They be staying in all winter, all during the snow. They don't be coming out when the hawk around. And you don't be seeing them when it rain. But come spring and summer they don't never seem to go in. They don't sleep or nothing. All they be doing is drinking that wine and bugging people, they always be trying to get something for nothing. Like bears be trying to take honey from little bees. When the bees done worked so hard to make it. But that's OK, 'cause sometimes the bears, they get stung."

Geraldine walked on through the park. "Oh! Those wild flowers, they beautiful! I'll take me some to Big Mama." She put the warm sweet bread down on a nearby bench. She pick a few yellow flowers. Then Geraldine saw this man coming up to her. She pick up the sweet bread and put the flowers on top of the bag.

The man walked up to the bench and say, "What's happening?"

Geraldine checked him out. He look like a hip old man.

She say. "I'm just picking me some of these flowers for my grandma."

"Most young folk don't be giving flowers. I'll help you pick some," the stranger say.

"Thanks, my grandma, she really dig flowers. She all the time say, "Give me flowers while I'm living. I can't smell them when I'm dead!"

"Talking 'bout smells…Hmmmm. Something sure do smell good."

"That my grandma's sweet bread. It do kind of smell good, don't it?"

"It sure do. It's a wonder bees ain't a swarming around. It smell sweet as honey. Can I walk you to your grandma's house? There's lots of people in the park today. You never know, somebody might try to snatch your sweet bread."

"Thank you. But no thank you. My mama told me not to be going nowhere with no stranger. It ain't far."

"Well, if you say so. It ain't far?"

"No. Just on Parker Street."

"Oh good. Near Donald's liquor store?"

"Yeah, two doors from it."

"Well, I know you got to get moving. Your grandma sure is a lucky lady to have a nice little girl like you."

"Thank you," Geraldine say as she walked on away.

Geraldine felt kind of scared. She didn't want to be losing her cool. So she walk kind of slow out the park, smelling the flowers. When she couldn't see the stranger no more, she ran like lightening. She went straight on to her grandma's house.

Geraldine told Big Mama what went on in the park. She told Big Mama how she tried to be cool, but how she was scared.

"Well, child. I'm glad you made it. You just met a bear trying to get some free honey. That's all."

"Oh," say Geraldine. But she didn't know what Big Mama was talkin 'bout.

"I wouldn't be a bit surprised if he ain't done followed you here," say Big Mama.

"Oh, no! I hope he ain't," say Geraldine.

"Hope is good, but it ain't enough. We got to help ourselves out."

"What we gonna do, a little girl and an old woman?" ask Geraldine.

"I'm old, but I ain't defenseless. Get me one of them empty wine bottles, my butcher knife, my skillet, my rolling pin and my Sunday hat pin, " say Big Mama.

"What you gonna do with them, Big Mama?"

"Use them—if we have to. We can be looking for him out this here window while we eat our sweet bread."

Old, But Not Defenseless: A Story in Transition

"Geraldine, I want you to take this here cold homemade wine to Big Mama. Go straight to her house. Don't tarry. You hear me?"

"Yes, Mama. I'll go straight there." Geraldine slipped on her brightly colored dashiki. The one Big Mama had got for her at the African store. And she was off with the wine to Big Mama's house. It was a beautiful day out. Spring was in the air. Flowers were blooming. Birds were singing. It was kind of hot, too. It was so hot Geraldine decided to take a short cut through the park where it was cool. Geraldine's mother didn't like for her to go through the park. Geraldine could hear her mother talking now. "Weird characters be hanging out in that park. You hear me? If you gotta go through it, go with some of your friends. And step fast, child. Don't stop for nothing at all. If some guy say something to you, say 'Hello,' but keep on stepping in the direction you going. It's always better to speak than not speak. Cause if you don't, they'll curse you out or go upside your head."

Geraldine was walking briskly through the park. Lots of people were lying on the grass and sitting on the benches.

Someone said, "Good afternoon, young lady. Where you going?"

She stopped in her tracks. She looked around to see where the voice was coming from. She saw a man about her grandfather's age.

Geraldine sized him up. He was raggedy, but clean. He didn't look dangerous. "He probably just a nosey, lonely man," she thought.

"I'm going to Big Mama's house on Pear Street."

"Oh, near the First Baptist Church?"

"Yeah, right next door to it. How did you know?"

"Well, I get around. I know some people who live over there."

"It's a small world, ain't it?" said Geraldine, trying to sound grown-up.

"Yes. I suppose you are taking that big bottle to your grandmother."

"Yes, I am."

"Something she likes?"

"Yes. Homemade wine."

"Wine," said the stranger. "Well, that's very nice." He picked a flower blossom from one of the nearby trees. "Let's give this to your grandmother," he said with a bow. "Thank you for talking to an old man."

"Thank you," said Geraldine as she walked away. "Ain't he a nice old man!" she thought.

The stranger had other thoughts. And they were not good ones. He planned to beat Geraldine to her grandmother's house. He could beat her there with no sweat. He had a suitcase hidden behind a nearby tree. He opened it up.

"Let's see now. What disguise should I use? I know! I'll be an elderly insurance man. Old people are always interested in life insurance. The old woman will welcome me in her house."

Quicker than Superman, he had his disguise on. It was a gray beard, a rumpled brown suit, and, of course, a briefcase. He started making tracks to Big Mama's house. As he walked, he thought about how good that wine would taste. The stranger went up the steps and rang the doorbell.

"Who there?" asked Big Mama.

"It's your friendly neighborhood insurance man," said the stranger.

"I don't want any! And I can't afford none!"

"We're giving away a free gift just for listening, Madam."

"Well, why didn't you say so? Just a minute. I got to press the buzzer to let you in."

The insurance man came inside the house. Grandmother said to him, "Lots of bums come around here. I got to be careful, me being an old woman."

"Yes, I can understand that, Madam. A lot of tramps and winos."

"Take a load off your feet."

The stranger sat down. He smiled at the old woman. Then he tapped his briefcase. He looked around as if he was expecting someone.

Big Mama was checking him out. "I ain't going to take my eyes off of him. I bet he ain't up to no good," she thought. Just then, the doorbell rang.

"Oh, that must be my grandchild."

"Hi, Big Mama. How you today?"

"Oh, just fine, child."

"I brought you some homemade wine."

"WINE!" said the stranger. His eyes bulged out. He smacked his lips. "WINE!"

"Yeah," say Big Mama. "It's for my blood. I needs iron."

"Oh, yeah? Well, I need it, too." The stranger jumped up and ran toward Geraldine to grab the wine.

He was quick, but Big Mama was quicker.

"Just what you think you doing? This here my wine!" said Big Mama with one hand on her hip and the other hand on the wine bottle.

"Wine, wine, wine!" said the thirsty, bug-eyed stranger.

"Do I look like a liquor store to you? Well, let me tell you, Mr. Insurance Man, that this here wine is mine. I may be old.

But I ain't defenseless. If you try to take my wine, you'll find out right quick I ain't defenseless. I'll crack this wine bottle upside your head before I'll let you have it. Geraldine, you use this broom here. Get me my big skillet out the kitchen, child."

"Now there you go getting mad. I was only funning, Sister. Can't you take a joke?" The stranger knew he was overpowered. "I'm gone." He picked up his briefcase and ran out the door.

What I Got to be Proud Of

In the AAL version of the story *What I Got to be Proud Of* a student tells a friend who just graduated what has been going on at school since the friend left. He relates an incident which results in a student and a teacher learning more about the accomplishments of Black people. The story also addresses the stigma attached to having dark skin.

The T version of the story follows the same story line as the AAL version, but is written in language closer to Standard English. There are fewer AAL features, such as the triple negatives that are, according to Smitherman, "The sole province of Africanized English," e.g. "Bloods ain't never done nothing worthwhile." There are changes in story details and events from the AAL version.

Booklet Three

Booklet Three is composed of two stories, *A Friend In Need* and *Dreamy Mae*. There are three versions of each story (AAL, T, SE). The students are helped by this structure to understand the relationship between their language and the language of school texts.

In the three versions of *A Friend in Need*, Russell, the main character in the story, has a car that looks good but runs poorly. He has an opportunity to use a garage free of charge, with all the tools he needs, but only between certain hours. In order to get the work done within the time limit he needs the help of a friend. In each version his friend arrives late and ruins the chance for him to repair his car. This story carries the themes of collaboration, social responsibility and the importance of being on time. The student is taken from AAL to T to SE. In the Transition version, the narration moves toward SE while the dialogue remains closer to AAL.

Dreamy Mae is about a student who constantly daydreams of being a princess with long golden hair. A newly found friend styles her hair and helps her feel that her hair is beautiful in its natural form. The three versions of *Dreamy Mae* address the cultural stigma of kinky or nappy hair. The story carries the theme "nappy hair is good hair." As in the case of *A Friend in Need*, the T version of *Dreamy Mae* continues to place strong emphasis on African American Language in the dialogue while the narration moves the student towards Standard English

Booklet Four

Booklet Four contains the stories *Little Big Man* and *Vibration Cornbread*, both written in T and SE. In the versions of *Little Big Man*, a student decides to drop out of school due to the family's economic condition. He needs to work more in order to support the family. This story addresses an economic reality for many Black families. In the T version there are fewer African American Language features. Movement toward Standard English is seen in both the narration and the dialogue. The SE version is written in textbook-style Standard English.

The story *Vibration Cornbread* addresses the Black cultural tradition of vibration cooking. The children in this story are putting what they learned from watching their mother to work. They are also learning responsibility. The children are what they label latch-key kids and are cooking dinner to surprise their mother.

As with *Little Big Man*, there are fewer African American Language features with movement toward Standard English evident in both the narration and the dialogue. The SE version is written in textbook-style Standard English.

Booklet Five

In Booklet Five, the sentence structure and vocabulary items are consistent with Standard English as written in school textbooks. From this point on the reading program is entirely in Standard English. Booklet Five contains four stories in SE, *I'll Always Remember*, *City Folks*, *Dig and be Dug in Return*, and *What Folks Call Politics*.

The story content in Booklet Five, as in all other Booklets, is about Black people living in a Black community. In the story, *I'll Always Remember*, Shannon, a young Black woman on her first trip to New York City, is conned into handing over her wallet to a "City Slicker."

I'll Always Remember: A Story in Standard English

"Today is my sixteenth birthday," thought Shannon Simms. She leaned on her elbow and looked out the train window. "I didn't know it would take this long to go from Connecticut to New York City." Shannon had looked forward to visiting her godfather in New York for a long time. She hadn't seen him for three years. For her birthday, he had sent her a round-trip ticket to New York.

"It will be good to be away from that country town for a whole week. I wonder what New York is like," Shannon said to herself. "New York, here I come!" She felt as though she were floating on a cloud.

"Last stop! New York!" said the train conductor.

Shannon got off the train. She walked to the baggage-claim section where people were pushing, shoving and pulling. She waited until everyone else had picked up their baggage. Then she put her coat over her arm and claimed her two bags. She walked outside to the taxi stand. There were no taxis in sight. Shannon sat on one of her bags while she waited. In this strange new city she felt very small.

A well-dressed man in his late twenties walked up to her. "Good morning. My name is William Henry," he said.

"Hello, my name is Shannon Simms."

"Pleased to meet you, Shannon. If you're waiting for a taxi, you'll have a long wait. They've all left for the city."

"Oh, my!" said Shannon.

"It's quicker and cheaper to take the subway," said William Henry.

"It is?"

"Yes! It's called the poor man's taxi," said Mr. Henry. "Where are your going?"

"To the Bronx."

"I'm going there too," said Mr. Henry. "I'll be happy to show you the way."

"Oh, thank you, Mr. Henry."

"Here, I'll help you carry your bags," Said Mr. Henry, as he picked up her largest bag.

They crossed the street and went down into the subway station. They got on the first train that arrived. It was as crowded as a can of sardines. So they had to stand.

"First time in New York?" asked Mr. Henry.

"Yes, it is," said Shannon.

"You have to watch out for city slickers. See the way you're carrying your purse? Someone could steal your wallet."

"Oh! I hope not. I have four hundred dollars in it. My family gave it to me for this trip."

"Well, you had better be very careful. Keep your purse close to your side."

"I will," said Shannon, as she tucked the purse closer under her arm.

"Yes, those city slickers are really slick," said Mr. Henry.

Some people got off at the next stop. Mr. Henry and Shannon found seats together. Shannon was still holding her purse close to her side.

"Are you sure you can manage your purse, coat and heavy bag?"

"Yes, I think so."

"Are you sure? Why don't you let me hold your wallet? If some slicker grabs your purse, you'll still have your wallet."

"But I'm holding my purse tightly."

"How are you going to carry your purse tightly with a heavy bag and a big coat? Here, let me hold your wallet. It'll be safer with me. I'll give it back to you when we leave the crowded subway."

"Well...OK," Shannon said, as she gave him her wallet.

William Henry told Shannon all about New York. He told her about movies and plays he had seen. About places to visit and places to eat. He told her how the city came alive at night.

"This is where we get off to change trains."

Shannon and William Henry walked upstairs to catch their train to the Bronx. The train platform was empty.

"I guess we just missed a train," said Mr. Henry.

"Yes, it sure is quiet."

Shannon looked up and down the tracks and listened for the train. She didn't know which way it would be coming from. William Henry looked around the platform. Then he said, "I'll go to that booth and ask the train attendant what time the train is due. I'll leave your bag here."

"Good idea," said Shannon.

"I'll be right back! You look and listen for the train in that direction," he said, pointing.

"OK."

Shannon looked, listened, and waited for the train. Then she turned towards the booth. She didn't see Mr. Henry. She saw only the man in the booth. She picked up her two bags and walked over to the booth.

"Did a man stop here to ask about the train?"

"No," said the train attendant, "I haven't talked to anyone for at least twenty minutes."

Shannon was puzzled. Then she thought, "Oh, no. William Henry, or whoever he was, has stolen my wallet! No, I gave it to him. He was a real city slicker. He tricked me. Now what am I going to do? I don't have a dime to my name."

• • •

The story *City Folks* tells of a country boy, Joey, new to the city while *Dig and be Dug in Return* is a story that takes on a poem by Langston Hughes

I play it cool and dig all jive
That's the reason I stay alive.
My motto, as I live and learn
Is dig and be dug in return.

As can be seen in the above excerpts, the stories in Booklet Five have a grammatical structure consistent with Standard English. The dialogue and the narration is that found in textbooks using Standard English. By the time the students reach Booklet Five the transition to Standard English is complete. The students have an understanding of the relationship between their oral language and the written ones used in Standard English text books.

Study Books

Each Reading Booklet is accompanied by a Study Book. The Study Books support the Reading Booklets by supplying instruction in reading and practice activities. The activities are composed of Story Questions, Skills Lessons and Word Bridging Lesson.

Story Questions

Each story has questions that correspond to the dialect that the story is written in (African American Language, Transition, and Standard English). These questions are designed to test the student's understanding of topics and details. For stories presented in multiple language versions, while the themes of the story remain unchanged from version to version, some details will vary. For example, the correct answer to the question, 'How much money did John receive?' could be, 'A whole lot of money' in the African American Language version, $800 in the Transition version, and $500 in the Standard English version.

Directions

The Story Questions are preceded by a set of directions. The directions convey to the students the message that they are valued and respected socially and culturally. For example, the story, *Shine*, begins, "Go for what you know about the story, *Shine*. Check out each sentence down below. Circle the letter of the correct answer (a, b, c, or d). There ain't but one right answer to each questions, so don't be picking out two" (Simpkins et al, 1977). The students have schemes of prior knowledge to contribute. The language of the directions coveys to the students that this knowledge is valid and acknowledged.

Skills Lessons

As in the above mentioned Story Questions, the Skills Lessons were written in the dialect of the corresponding short story. The lessons were designed to assist students with their comprehension and application of reading skills.

The authors identified nine skills they believed to be vital for bridging the gaps in the students' learning. These included: meaning from context, figures of speech, key meaning words, word order, time order, word parts, inference, main idea, and cause and effect. These skills were retaught, refined, and extended in the three dialects.

The design of the Skills Lessons reflects the authors' emphasis on the search process in the Bridge Reading Program. The search process is more important than obtaining the right answers by mass practice. The student is provided with a limited number of questions and asked to find the answers at their own pace. The Skills Lessons focus on getting the student to understand the underlying concepts (in this particular vernacular). The students are allowed to relearn how to read in a non-threatening, supportive social environment conducive to learning. The Skills Lesson for *Shine*, entitled "Digging on Figures of Speech" exemplifies the above.

Digging on Figures of Speech

What you gon learn from this:

To dig on words that say more than what the words really mean.

Check this out:

You got a figure of speech when you come across a word, or some words, that ain't really saying what it seem to be saying. To understand this here figure-of-speech thing, to really get it together, you got to use a little taste of imagination. You can't be using the exact meaning of the words. What you got to do is trip on the picture that the words paint for you.

Now check this example:

- Shine *shot on off through the water like a motorboat.*

Now, if you was to say, "Shine *shot on off through the water* like a motorboat," what would you be saying? Now, you wouldn't be saying he was a bullet. And you wouldn't be getting down on him, saying he look like a boat. You'd be saying that the Brother could swim like crazy. Or that the Brother was a super swimmer. Or that the Brother could swim real fast. You understand what we're trying to say?

Now check this:

- The whale say, "I'm *king of the ocean.* I'm *king of the sea.*"

Now, if you was to say you was *king of the ocean,* what would you be saying? Now, you wouldn't be saying you was the main man of some country. And you wouldn't be saying there was a ruler just for the ocean. You'd be saying you was the strongest and baddest thing that live in the ocean.

Let's put this stuff to work for you:

Dig on the words that's underlined. Pick out what the underlined words really say. Then circle the letter in front of the words. One is already done to show you how.

- Shine *split* back up on deck. He say, "This ship is sinking."

    a. Shine fell apart.
    b. *Shine moved quickly.*
    c. Shine started crying.

1. Winds, storms, icebergs—nothing could *fade it*.

    a. Nothing could go alongside it.
    b. Nothing could get behind it.
    c. *Nothing could harm it.*

2. This ship was the *biggest, baddest, coldest and the boldest ship ever to sail*.

    a. *No other ships could match it.*
    b. It was hard to get along with.
    c. It had a bad understanding.

3. The ship was *out of sight*!

    a. It was off in the distance and you couldn't see it.
    b. *It was the best ship ever built.*
    c. It was hidden in the fog.

4. The ship could *move like a posse running from a drive-by*.

    a. *It was a real fast ship.*
    b. It was a real slow ship.
    c. It was a black ship.

The Standard English versions of the Skills Lessons have a more formal, textbook-style tone to them. They represent what the student must master in order to be successful in school. The following questions are excerpted from the "Understanding Figures of Speech" section for *A Friend in Need*.

Understanding Figures of Speech

What you will learn:

To understand words that mean more than what they seem to say. Circle the letter of the words that mean the same as the underlined words in each sentence. One is done to show you how.

- James Russell *loved his car like a baby loves milk.*

    a. He really liked his car.
    b. He really hated his car.
    c. He didn't care about his car.

1. That engine is *as overdue as last month's rent.*

    a. It is in excellent shape.
    b. It is in need of repair.
    c. It is owed to the landlord.

2. Russell thanked Joe. He drove out of the gas station *sounding like a round of machine-gun fire.*

    a. He drove noisily.
    b. He drove quietly.
    c. He drove carelessly.

3. Russell was as *angry as a bull in a bullfight.*

    a. He was very pleased.
    b. He was very upset.
    c. He was a little upset.

4. Willie jumped in the car as *quick as a flash.*

    a. He jumped very slowly.
    b. He jumped very carefully.
    c. He jumped very fast.

Word Bridging Lessons

Students are provided with an exercise designed to improve their vocabulary. These lessons help the students to translate back and forth between African American Language and Standard English. Then students are taught synonym recognition. The stories assist the students in defining word meanings in both language versions.

Word Bridging (African American Language Version)

What you gon learn:

How to tighten up your reading by knowing a whole lot of words. Look at the numbered sentences. And look at the list of the Bridging Words. Sometime you gon find just words on the list. Sometime you gon find groups of words or word phrases on the list. Ya heard?

Now you ready to begin:

The first thing you gotta do is read a sentence and think about what the italicized word mean. Then check out the list of Bridging Words. Next:

- Pick out two words or word phrases from the list that mean just about the same thing as the word that's italicized in the sentence.
- Write one of the words or word phrases in the first box. Write the other word or word phrase in the other box.
- Cross the words you used off the list so you can't use them again.
- Now think of some more words that mean almost the same thing as the italicized word. These words ain't on the list. They words you know already. Write them on the two blank lines under the boxes.

- Tell whether your words are African American Language or Standard English.

Now that's all you gotta do, and that ain't hard, is it? The first one is done for you. If you don't understand, ask your teacher to help you.

Bridging Words

enjoyment	attention
~~Afro-American female~~	reflecting on
criticizing	thought
dancing	pleasure
~~Black woman or girl~~	reprimanding
strength	appreciating

- This here little *Sister* name Mae was most definitely untogether.
  Sister

Afro-American female	Black woman or girl
Negro woman or girl–SE	woman of African ancestry–SE

1. Her teacher was always *getting on* her bout dreaming in class.
   getting on

criticizing	reprimanding

2. Mae didn't pay them no mind. She kept *tripping on* her daydream.
   tripping on

reflecting on	appreciating

3. I guess daydreaming was her *thang*.

thang

pleasure		enjoyment	

4. Two girls walked on away laughing and singing, "Nappy head girl, just dream all day." Mae didn't pay them no *mind*.

mind

attention		thought	

Word Bridging (Standard English Version)

What you will learn:

How to improve your reading by learning some new words. Look at the numbered sentences. And look at the list of the Bridging Words. Sometimes there will be just words on the list. Sometimes there will be groups of words or word phrases on the list.

Now you're ready to begin:

First, read a sentence and think about what the italicized word means. Then look through the list of Bridging Words. Next:

- Pick out two words or word phrases from the list that mean just about the same thing as the word that's italicized in the sentence.
- Write one of the words or word phrases in the first box. Write the other word or word phrase in the other box.
- Cross the words you used off the list so you can't use them again.
- Now think of some more words that mean almost the same thing as the italicized word. These words aren't on the list.

They're words you know already. Write them on the two blank lines under the boxes.

- Tell whether your words are African American Language or Standard English.

That's all there is to it. The first italicized word is done as an example. If you need help, ask your teacher.

Bridging Words

split	together
~~tripping~~	cracked up
foxy	run it down
busted their sides	stepped fast
~~grooving~~	chunked
crazy	ditched

- Mae was *daydreaming* about being a princess.
  daydreaming

tripping	grooving

  spacing out–AAL   fantasizing–SE

1. The boys and girls *ran* outside to play ball.
   ran

split	stepped fast

2. Mae *dropped* her sandwich in the garbage can.
   dropped

ditched	chunked

3. "Ha, ha," her classmates *laughed*. They didn't believe Mae would ever be a princess.

laughed

cracked up	busted their sides

---

4. Mae was as *dreamy* as the Black princess.

dreamy

together	foxy

Starting the Program

The students are introduced to the program by way of an audio recording played for the entire class. The narrator on the audio is a Black male, speaking in African American Language. By speaking in what the students can immediately identify as familiar language the social, cultural and linguistic traditions of the Black community are connected. The narrator welcomes the students with a communal greeting — "What's happening, Brothers and Sisters."

The narrator then addresses students' fears and concerns about reading related to their resistance to school instruction. The narrator explains the language used in the program. The students are told that the program makes a distinction between the language that they speak and the language of the school and the text books. They are told that they will start in African American Language and 'end up' in Standard English.

"Well anyway, in this hear program, you start off with
what we call soul talk. You know, the way you hear a
lot of Blacks talk. We call this talk African American
Language. You got that? Soul talk and African American Language is the same thing. And end up in Standard English. Now you know what Standard English
is, don't you? That's what you see in the text books,
or you hear on radio and TV and the way you hear
the teacher talk, and stuff like that. You know."

The students are introduced to the stories and Skill Lessons
by way of an audio- tape, then follow a transcript of the introduction to the story *Shine*, and Skill Lessons.

Introduction to Reading Story:
Shine A Story in African American Language

This recording is for the story called *Shine*. You got that? *Shine*.
You ought to have your reading booklet open to this story now.
The story *Shine* come from Black folklore. You understand? Black
folklore is stories that folks use to tell and sing a long time ago.

This story is about a dynamic Brother who had his thing together so much, he just turned everything all around in his favor.
You see, it started out like this. The Brother was nothing but a
hard working flunky. Shoveling coals with a whole lot of soul to
these engines on this here great big out-of-sight ship, the *Titanic*.
Then one day, while the ship was traveling along the ocean, it
started leaking real bad and the only one who really knew what
was happening was this Brother called Shine. He tried to hip the
captain to the trouble, but the captain, he didn't wanta be hearing
none of this. Wasn't going for it. He didn't wanta be listening to
no Shine. He didn't think Shine had enough sense to know
anything.

Now the ship was definitely sinking and Shine was the only one who knew this. And since nobody wanted to listen to him, he decided he wasn't going for this. You know, sho nuff, man, he wasn't going to be hanging around here and be going down with this boat. So he decided it was time for him to go on and make his move. You understand? He was gon do something. When it all came down, the Brother had everybody begging him to help them.

And what you think about that? What you think cause this big change-around? What you think the Brother did? And when you read the story, you will find out what went down. But before you read it, I'm gonna run down and see where it is that might hang you up.

Now look at the words on the first page of the story *Shine*. When I say each word, what you got to do is just look at them and try to remember them. OK? This first word is **Titanic**, you got that? **Titanic**. The next is **superbad**. Yeah, **superbad**. Number three is **iceberg**. **Iceberg**. The fourth word is **unsinkable**. **Unsinkable**. The fifth word is **Shoveling**. **Shoveling**. The next one is **Stoker**. **Stoker**. The seventh one is **survivors**. **Survivors**. The eighth word is **furnace**. **Furnace**. The ninth word is **mercy**. **Mercy**. The last word is **squeezing**. **Squeezing**.

Now read this story by yourself. When you finish, do the Story Questions in your Study Book. Now remember now, you get any kind of hang-ups at all, don't be bashful. Go and raise your hand up. The teacher is going to be helping you.

Introduction to Skills Lesson:
Shine, A Story in African American Language

You ought to have your Study Book open to the Skills Lesson for the story *Shine*. It's a story in African American Language. Since you already read this story, you ready to do the Skills Lesson. Now listen close to what I tell you. I'm gonna read this whole

Skills Lesson, and you suppose to read it along with me. If you
don't understand something, go back and listen to it again. If you
still don't understand, ask the teacher. Understand?

(Skills Lesson for *Shine* is read in full here)

Now put this recording away and do the exercise in the Skills
Lesson. After you finish, take your work to your teacher.

Teacher's Guide

The Teacher's Guide contains extensive background on the problem
and teaching information. Included in the Teacher's Guide is a step
by step lesson plan which instructs them on how to implement the
program. The Guide also contains transcripts of the recordings and
a glossary of African American Language terms used in the readers.

Peer Control

Peer Control reading can be classified as another Skill Lesson
component. It provides a safe social environment for the students to relearn how to read. In the Peer Controls small group
students are allowed to work collaboratively, interact socially and
support one another. The procedures draw heavily on the call
and response-oral tradition of the Black community. Teachers
and students found Peer Control to be the most enjoyable part of
the program. Separate stories are used for Peer Control. Peer
controls follow the Associative Bridging sequence.

Updating Bridge 2

The Bridge reading program has been revised and expanded following the cross-cultural approach outlined in this book. Bridge 2:
A Cross-Cultural Reading Program (Simpkins, Smitherman, Stalling, 2002) is currently available to researchers who wish to replicate the original data (Houghton Mifflin, 1976) in public schools.

The language used in Bridge 2 was updated after a series of linguistic field studies in prder to match current usage by the target population. In a number of the stories, the subject matter has also been updated in order to reflect more current topics of interest. The following story, excerpted from Booklet One of Bridge 2 is an example of the types of changes to the reading program.

Old School Rap Part One, Gangsta Rap and the Black Oral Tradition: A Story in African American Language

It was Saturday bout one. The whole crew was kicking it in front of J-Dogg's pad. They was just chilling and making up rap songs. You know, getting down with some gangsta rap, working on their rhymes. J-Dogg's grandfather came out the house with a brown paper bag.

Grandmaster Willie D say, "What's up Pops?"

"Don't be calling me no Pops. I'll pop you upside your head youngblood."

"What's in the bag?" Little J asked.

"My tonic," Pops say. "My toddy for my body."

"I heard that," Little 2Sweet say. "Man gotta have his medicine with him at all times."

"What you all doing hanging around here? Looking for somebody to mug?"

"We ain't into no crime, Grandpa, we into rap," J-Dogg say. "Come on, cut us some slack, this is my crew, Grandpa. When we get over, and we living large, I'm gon take care of you, Grandpa. Check this out. Give me a beat, Grandmaster Willie D!"

> *We was chilling in the hood*
> *And everything was good*
> *We don't do no time*

cause we ain't into crime
But if you dis us, we got our 9's.

Grandpa listened a little while, then he shook his head and say, "Is that the best you can do? That's wack."

"Check it, Grandpa," J-Dogg say, making fun of him. "We didn't know you was into gangsta rap and hip-hop."

Grandpa say, "Be-bop, hip-hop, it's all the same. I was down with rap before you was even born. You don't know nothing about nothing."

"I heard that! Word, Pops. Give us the 4-1-1 on rap. Tell us about the Old School," Grandmaster Willie D say, as everybody start laughing again.

"What you laughing about you little punks. Let me educate your dumb butt. Let me run it down for you."

Everybody sat down on the porch and Grandpa started to preach. He took a drink from his bottle and then he say, "It all got started back there in Africa. You see, back then they didn't write nothing down. They would make up and tell stories about things that was important to them. They would tell stories about they land, the baddest warriors, the mightiest of hunters and all them good things. They would be sitting around the village campfire, somebody would get down with a bad beat, and then they would tell stories about they history. They would pass the stories on from generation to generation. It was called the Black Oral Tradition. You got that? The Black Oral Tradition. Now gangsta rap, it got started in this country a long time ago. And it's all part of the Black Oral Tradition.

"Most of it was made up by inmates who was in prison or jail. They had a whole lot of time on their hands and nothing to do. So they made up stories about the life. The sporting life, the street life, the fast life. The stories was bout bad men,

tricksters, pimps, lovers and all that. They called them toasts.
What they was, was long and short narratives. They was in
rhyme and they was metered. You couldn't be just saying the
words. You had to have style! You had to put on a show! A
performance!

"Word up, Pops!" 2Sweet say. "Bust a move, put on a
show for us. Unless you think it's too wack."

"Too wack? Dig on this youngblood."

> *My woman cried, she almost died*
> *When I made off with her mink*
> *But I stayed my role, and I stole and I stole*
> *Everything but the kitchen sink.*
> *"That's he, that's he!"*
> *she shouted with glee*
> *That's the smooth talkin' man, with the gangsta plan*
> *That made a street walker out of me.*

They all started paying attention real good. Grandpa was
getting into it. Really putting on a show. The crew was taking it all in, and it was all good. The more he did, the more he
got into it, the more the group liked it. After drinking some
more, he started in again.

> *Now attorney Spence headed up Bud's defense*
> *He was known as an all time great,*
> *And in his hand, Bud put 2 grand*
> *And on his skill Bud risked his fate.*
> *"I can't beat this rap," Spence said as he counted his*
>   *bread.*
> *"The politicians just won't buy*
> *DA Pace has an airtight case*
> *And I can't bribe the FBI."*

After a while, Grandpa stopped and drunk some more of his tonic. The crew say, "Don't be stopping now, go on, please! It's getting good. Go on with the toast."

He tells bout how Bud goes in front of the judge and gets 5 to 10. And when the judge asks if he got anything to say, Grandpa closes the toast with:

> *I ain't crying cause the agent was lying*
> *And left you with the notion*
> *That I was a big wheel in the narcotics field*
> *I hope that lame cops a promotion.*
> *It's all the same, it's all in the game*
> *I knew that when I sat down to play*
> *You take all the odds, deal all the low cards*
> *That's dues a playa must pay.*
> *5 to 10 that ain't no time*
> *I got a brother in Sing Sing doing 99.*

By the time Pops got finished, a whole lot of young people had come into the group. J-Dogg say, "Come on, Grandpa, do some more for us."

Pops say, "Well, let's go on in the backyard." Everybody moved to the backyard cause there was more room. Moms fixed some refreshments. She brought out Kool-Aid, cookies and some chips.

Pops was running it down to the kids about the kind of folks who made up the toasts. Pops say, "They didn't have what you got going for you now. Most of them didn't have no schooling, and if they did, it was just to the third or fourth grade. Almost none of them ever finished high school. And college was a place where white people and a few rich Black people went. The life, the street life, was all they knew. Now

I ain't saying that there wasn't no hard working Black folks who didn't go into the life.

"I mean, like there was plenty of Black people who made the best of what they had. Plenty of God fearing people that raised good families. But for the people we talking about, the street life was all they knew, and they loved it. They knew they probably was gon spend most of they lives behind bars or worse. But they loved the life." Pops say, "Now that's all. I got to take care of my business."

J-Dogg say, "Come on, Grandpa, just one more."

Everyone started begging for one more. They say, "You the man, just lay one more on us."

Pops say, "OK, but this the last one. Like I done told you, I got bidness to take care of."

Everybody gathered round. Pops continued:

Once I lived the life of a millionaire
I spent my money like I just didn't care
When I was rich, and things were right
I used to spend my money like I was white.
I took my friends out and showed them a real
    good time.
I bought them good food, whiskey, and the best wine.
But now that I'm out of it and feeling so low
I ain't got no friends and no place to go.
I asked a friend to help me, I needed something
    to eat.
He say, "Get out my face, you homeless chump,
    hit the mission down the street!"
That's when I learned what it was all about.
Nobody cares bout you when you're down and out.

Now that I'm back on my feet
Many an old friend I chance to meet.
They say, "How you doin' old pal of mine!
What's the chance of you lending me a dime?"
I say, "Before you can get a dime of mine
You got to show me you crazy, crippled, and blind
You got to have both legs cut off at the knees
And suffer from TB and heart disease.
You got to show me a doctor's note written in red
That your momma, children, and wife all dead.
You got to show me an elephant nesting in trees.
And poor people who don't eat black-eyed peas.
And if you show me all this in record time,
I might loan you a nickel, but I won't loan you a
        dime."

9

Implementing the Bridge Program

The implementation of the *Bridge Program* can be divided into three components: (a) Structured Sequence and Flow of Materials, (b) The Role of the Teacher, and (c) Management of the Peer Control Procedure.

Sequence and Flow of Materials

Students using the *Bridge Program* follow a basic four-step sequence that repeats itself as they move through the various materials. This sequence allows the students to proceed at their own individual pace without reference to the other students in the classroom. The basic four-step sequence is described below.

Step 1: Tapes

The student selects the tape that corresponds to the story that she is to read and a tape recorder from its designated location. The student returns to her desk and listens to the taped abstract of the story as many times as she wishes. If there are things that the student does not understand on the tape, the student raises her hand for assistance from the teacher. When the student finishes listening to the tape, she rewinds it and returns the tape and the recorder to their locations.

Step 2: Individual Reading

Upon returning the tape and the recorder, the student takes the reading selection which corresponds to the tape, returns to his desk and reads it as many times as he wants. If there are things he does not understand in the selection or that present difficulty for him, the student raises his hand for assistance from the teacher. Then the student finishes reading the selection and returns it to its original location.

Step 3: Story Questions

Upon returning the reading selection, the student selects a sheet and the story questions which correspond to the reading material she just finished. The student then returns to her desk and proceeds to answer the story questions, indicating her answers on the worksheet. After answering all the questions, she checks her answers against the correct ones provided on the back of the Story Question sheet. The student records the number of correct answers on her Student Feedback Record.

Step 4: Skills

After recording his scores in the Feedback Record, the student returns the Story Question Sheet and takes the Skill Exercise that corresponds with the reading selection. The student returns to his seat and proceeds to work on the skill exercise. The first time the skills are taught, the student listens to a recording of the skill lesson and silently reads along with the recording. In the succeeding lessons, the student does the lessons without the aid of the recording.

When the student has completed the Skill Lesson, he takes it to the teacher to be corrected and to have the work individually reviewed. The student then records the number of correct answers on the Feedback Record. The student then completes a

Word Bridging Lesson corresponding to the reading material. The Word Bridging Lesson may be done as homework and returned to the teacher later for corrections.

Upon completion of Step Four, the student returns to Step One and repeats the sequence with another reading selection. The sequence is interrupted two days a week for Peer Control Reading Lessons.

This sequence, as outlined, varies only according to the availability of materials and recording equipment, the packaging of materials and the physical dimension of the classroom.

The Roles of the Teacher

The teacher assumes three roles in the *Bridge Program*: (a) manager of classroom behavior, (b) manager of materials, and (c) individual learning consultant. It is important that the teacher always remember the three roles. In this approach, **the roles are not intended to supplement the traditional roles of the teacher; they are intended to replace them.**

The old English schoolmaster is stereotypically pictured as a stern disciplinarian. The schoolmaster would not tolerate any misbehavior from his students. He would punish those who dared to misbehave (exhibit off-task behavior) or inadvertently misbehaved in order to set an example for the rest of the class. The other students would behave in the proper manner (stay on task) in order to avoid punishment. The schoolmaster was forever on the alert to catch the students misbehaving (off task) or being "bad." Whenever the schoolmaster caught one of them in the act, he would immediately punish that student. The schoolmaster's emphasis was focused on the negative (off task behavior) in order to achieve the positive (on task behavior). He generally ignored positive behavior or good behavior because it was expected of all students. The reward for positive behavior was avoidance of punishment.

A contrast can be drawn between the role of the English school-master and the role of the teacher in the *Bridge Program*. While the schoolmaster focused on the negative (off task behavior) and ignored the positive (on task behavior), the teacher in this approach does the exact opposite. The teacher focuses on the positive (on task behavior) and ignores, whenever possible, the negative (off task behavior). The teacher using the *Bridge Program* must be constantly on the alert for on task behavior in order to immediately praise or reinforce it. In this approach, the teacher must work hard at catching the student being "good," in order to disperse positive reinforcement.

In the role of manager of materials, the teacher supervises the distribution, use and flow of materials. It is the teacher's job to insure that the materials are used properly, in the manner in which they were designed to be used, and in the correct sequence.

As an individual learning consultant, the teacher works with one student at a time. As the term "individual learning consultant" indicates, the teacher consults with individual students on any learning problem or difficulty they might experience pertaining to materials used in the *Bridge Program*.

Manager of Classroom Behavior

The best reading program cannot be effective if there is a high frequency of disruptive behavior in the classroom. The best of teachers cannot be effective if a large portion of the available time is spent disciplining instead of teaching. When teachers are forced to assume the role of classroom police officer, learning is severely inhibited.

Although very little information is available on "Time on Task" in the literature as it relates to Black non-mainstream students, it is one of the most important variables related to school outcomes. Time on Task can be defined as the amount of time the teacher spends in the classroom on subject matter or curriculum activities as opposed to disciplinary activities.

As stated above, the best of teachers cannot be effective when a high percentage of their time is spent controlling, or attempting to control, disruptive behavior in the classroom. In schools where a great deal of learning is taking place and students are scoring well on standardized tests, we find that the Time on Task averages from 90 to 95%. In the typical inner-city school where the students are scoring low on such tests, the Time on Task varies between 20 to 65% (these figures are based on my observations and verbal reports received from teachers). This discrepancy illustrates a dramatic difference in the amount of instruction students at mainstream and non-mainstream schools receive.

The *Bridge Program* places a great deal of emphasis on increasing the Time on Task for Black non-mainstream students. This is achieved by: (1) Adding greater structure to the classroom, (2) having the teacher focus on dispensing reinforcement for on task behavior and (3) engaging the students with reading materials that reflects their language, culture, and interests.

The *Bridge Program* attempts to establish a success arena for Black students, a positive environment for learning. As Black students experience success, they begin to believe in themselves and in their ability to learn to read well, thereby enhancing their self-image. Most teachers are concerned about building a positive self-image in students, but they are also unsure of how to go about it. Generally, a poor self-image is the result of a perceived history of failure and unsatisfying experiences. Positive self-images result when a person perceives his experiences as successful and satisfying.

The following procedures are designed to help students achieve experiences of success. For these procedures to be effective, the teacher must use and practice **all** of them **consistently** and **exclusively**. They fall into two general categories: (a) collaborative rule setting, and (b) reinforcement of on task behavior.

Collaborative Rule Setting

When students have a consistent, familiar pattern to follow, they can operate more efficiently. The teacher's first task is to see that a set of rules is established to govern the behavior of the class. When students are involved in establishing these rules, they become more personal and meaningful. When not involved, there is danger of the rules being viewed as oppressive or as the establishment's impinging upon the students. For rules to be established collaboratively, the teacher and the students must make joint input. The class cannot establish any rule which the teacher does not agree with, nor can the teacher establish a rule which the class does not agree with. Agreement on the rules is reached through dialog and discussion. Past experience has shown that a dialog on "why do we need rules anyway" is an excellent starting point.

When engaged in collaborative rule setting or changing existing rules, the teacher should keep the following points in mind:

1. Keep the rules simple, short and to the point.
2. Phrase the rules in positive behavioral terms: "Sit quietly while working" instead of "Don't talk to your neighbor."
3. Make sure the students understand the purpose of the rules and their relationship to the goals of the classroom.

Once the rules are established, the teacher should post them in a highly visible location and review them regularly with the class.

Reinforcement

Research has demonstrated that when behavior is closely followed by attention, praise, or any other satisfying state for the learner, the behavior is strengthened and reinforced. When the reinforcement comes from something besides the intrinsic pleasure of the behavior, it is called extrinsic reinforcement. Extrinsic reinforcement, sometimes called extrinsic incentives, is reinforcement from an observable source external to the learner.

In the Cross-Cultural Approach, the teacher is constantly on the alert for desirable and on task behavior in order to immediately reinforce it. The following guide to extrinsic reinforcement was designed to be carefully and consistently followed by the teacher:

1) Praise: Reward each student who is on task (following the rules and working on assigned tasks) with praise. Do not reward students who are not on task, since attention, even for misbehavior, is rewarding. Praise can be a highly effective reinforcer. Praise following on task behavior tends to keep the student working on assigned tasks. Be constantly alert for opportunities to reinforce students for being on task. A smile, a nod, or some special remark can serve as a reinforcer. Make statements of praise personal. Praise can lose its effectiveness as a reinforcer if it becomes mechanical and impersonal.

2) Extinction: When behavior is not followed by reinforcement, the frequency of the behavior tends to decrease. This process is called extinction. Whenever possible, inappropriate behavior should be ignored. When a student intentionally breaks a rule or is not working on the assigned task, the teacher should ignore the student if possible. Continue to praise those students in the class who are on task.

   Remember, reinforcement for inappropriate behavior can and often does come from a student's classmates. Therefore, the teacher must have the aid of the entire class in ignoring inappropriate behavior. If the teacher is consistent, the class will also ignore inappropriate behavior. At first, the teacher will probably experience a temporary increase in the student's misbehavior. This is a test to see whether the teacher "really means it"— if she will consistently ignore inappropriate behavior and praise only appropriate or on task behavior.

3) Negative Reinforcement: Negative reinforcement, according to Skinner, is the removal of an aversive or noxious

(unpleasant) stimulus, thereby creating a rewarding state of affairs for the learner. If there are unpleasant conditions in the classroom, their removal can set a reinforcer, having the same approximate effect as a positive reinforcement, the strengthening of behavior.

A negative reinforcer is defined as a stimulus, the removal or avoidance of which increases a response. The example cited earlier in this section, of the schoolmasters's method of controlling behavior, is an example of negative reinforcement. The students behaved in the proper manner in order to avoid an aversion stimulus (punishment).

4) Disapproval: Sometimes it will be necessary to show disapproval, called punishment in learning theory terminology. Disapproval is not recommended except in extreme circumstances. Although punishment can suppress unwanted behavior, it does not eliminate it from the repertoire of the person engaging in the unwanted behavior and it may produce side effects seen as anxiety, aggression, or withdrawal.

The teacher will have to use his own judgment as to when and what kinds of inappropriate behavior can no longer be ignored, i.e., when a student might be injured, furnishings or materials destroyed, or the learning situation totally disrupted. If punishment is resorted to, it should be swift, fair and convey serious disapproval. Mild reprimands may serve only to reward the student for getting attention. When the teacher deems it necessary to employ punishment, he should be on the alert to restore praise at the earliest possible opportunity.

5) Intrinsic Reinforcement: When the behavior or activity a person engages in is done for its own sake rather than for an external reward (i.e. the activity itself creates a satisfying state of affairs for the learner), a state of intrinsic reinforcement is

achieved. Students learning for the pleasure of learning is the goal that the teacher should seek to move towards. If the use of extrinsic reinforcement is successful, the teacher will notice that fewer and fewer external rewards are necessary to encourage the students to engage in learning behavior.

What the Teacher Should Remember

Errors on the part of the teacher will be serious setbacks. They occur if the teacher breaks the rules. Another serious problem is making exceptions to the rules. This encourages the students to gamble on when the rules will not be applied. The teacher must always be consistent in applying the rules.

A primary source of extrinsic reinforcement for the misbehaving student is attention from peers, in the form of smiles, laughter and verbal encouragement, for example. The effect of such reinforcement is to increase frequency of behavior. Praise those who refuse to react to such behavior. Immediately praise the student when they get back on task. The cooperation of the class is one of the teacher's greatest assets in maintaining the learning situation.

Manager of Materials

The teacher's role as manager of materials can be a relatively simple task or it can become a frustrating chore. For the program to be successful, the teacher's first objective must be to immediately accustom the students to the structure of the learning sequence. In order for the students to work independently, they must first learn the structural sequence until they automatically adhere to it. If the suggested approach is followed, the teacher can accomplish this task with relative ease. She will need to apply the techniques in the previous section, Manager of Classroom Behavior. Again, the key word is consistency.

The arrangement of materials is crucial to the success of the *Bridge Program*. There are several key procedures the teacher must follow:

1. Consistently place the materials in the same location each day.
2. Make the students aware of the designated location of the materials. Review the location often.
3. Make each student aware of where to obtain the materials, what to do with them, and where to return them, before actually starting the program.
4. The students must know the sequence for using the materials. Generously praise students for using materials correctly and following the sequence.
5. Always have the materials in their designated place when the students arrive so that they can immediately begin to work.

Individual Learning Consultant

Most teachers are accustomed to working with groups of students rather than individuals. Usually their training and their placement in the school focus on group instruction. Teachers usually agree that individual instruction is more effective, but the materials generally available to them and the large numbers of students in their classes often make individual instruction almost impossible.

In the *Bridge Program*, the bulk of the teacher's time is devoted to the individual student rather than the group. In the role of individual learning consultant, the teacher works with students on an individual basis when they are encountering learning problems. When answering a student's question, the teacher, rather than giving the student the correct answer, consults with the student on how to develop strategies for independently deriving the answer. The teacher assists the student in understanding why certain answers are correct and others are not. For example, students will frequently need help deciphering unfamiliar words. When the teacher is asked for assistance, she helps the student use context or another decoding technique covered in the Skill Exercises. The teacher does not simply tell a student what the word means.

Management of Peer Control Procedure

Peer Control is an oral reading procedure designed for small groups of students. Students engaging in the Peer Control Procedure use Peer Control Reading selections. The reading materials used for this procedure follow the same format as the reading materials used in the structural sequence; i.e. three dialects and five steps. Each sentence of the Peer Control reading selection is numbered in order to facilitate assignment of reading passages (see Appendix for examples). The Peer Control content is not restricted to the Peer Control Reading Selections. Once students complete the Associative Bridging sequence, the Peer Control activity can be continued by using newspapers, magazines, and books.

General Peer Control Procedures

Grouping

Students are divided into small groups of four to six for the Peer Control reading activities. Students are grouped as closely as possible in terms of reading level in order to increase the probability of success for each student in a group. The groups should remain flexible so that students can be reassigned to a more appropriate group if their reading ability change.

Reading

Once the students are divided into groups, the activities proceed with the students conducting their own groups. The teacher designates the number of sentences each student will read and shows each group how to get started. Then the teacher acts only as a consultant to the group.

While one student (the Reader) reads aloud, the other students (the Correctors) follow the Reader silently. If the Correctors hear the Reader make an error, they stop the Reader. The Reader is then given a chance to recognize and correct the error. If the Reader cannot do so, the Correctors point out the error and explain how to correct it. The Reader must then start reading again from the beginning of his selection. When the Reader reads the assigned sentences without being stopped for an error, another student becomes the Reader and the first Reader becomes a Corrector. This procedure is repeated as the students take turns during the Peer Control Reading period.

Selecting the Readers

Occasionally problems may arise concerning who should read next. How such problems are resolved is up to the judgment of the teacher. Sometimes it is useful to use some method of random selection. One such method uses a set of numbered discs or slips of paper and a box, cup or other container. Students each choose a disc before the group begins the day's activity. They make a note of their own numbers and return the discs to the container. The student with the lowest number becomes the first Reader. When the first Reader finishes, she selects the next reader by choosing a disc from the container. The student with the number of the disc becomes the next Reader. In this way, each Reader chooses the next.

Peer Control Reading Skills Objectives

Peer Control allows students to practice and demonstrate knowledge of reading skills by (a) stopping the reader whenever reading errors are made, (b) indicating where and what kind of errors are made, and (c) assisting the reader to correct errors, if necessary. Students are taught how to spot specific kinds of reading errors. Once introduced, identification and correction of each error is reviewed and practiced in every succeeding reading selection. The errors to be identified are explained below. The teacher may choose to add additional errors to the list.

Non-Recognition of Words

This problem occurs when the student does not recognize or know a word. The student cannot attack a word at all.

Incorrect Recognition of Words

This error usually occurs when there is not a visual relationship between the written word and the student's response. The student may misread part of the word or the whole word. For example:

dig read as "gig" *what* read as "went"

was read as "saw" *strain* read as "string"

summertime read as "sometime"

Incorrect recognition of words does **not** include mispronunciation due to dialect differences. If a student pronounces "door" as "doe" or "store" as "stoe," it should be considered correct. If the teacher is uncertain of the African American Language pronunciation of a word, they should call upon the students in the peer control group as authorities on the correct dialect pronunciation. It is very important that African American Language pronunciations **not** be mistaken for reading errors.

Punctuation Errors

It is considered an error when the student does not read with the inflection appropriate to the punctuation. Punctuation in this case includes periods, commas, question marks, and exclamation marks.

Omission Errors

This problem occurs when the student omits complete words from the reading passage.

> Example: She had to split 'cause it was getting late.
> Read as: She had to split, it was getting late
> The word 'cause was omitted.

Insertion Errors

This occurs when the student adds words to reading passages.

> Example: Shine was a strong Brother
> Read as: Shine was a big strong Brother.
> The word big was inserted.

Substitution Errors

A substitution occurs when the student reads one word for another.

> Example: I'm going to my pad.
> Read as: I'm going to my house.
> The word house was substituted for pad.

If a Corrector spots legitimate reading errors other than the six types described above, they should be treated in the same way. The Reader should try to identify and correct the error first. If the Reader is unsuccessful, then the Corrector identifies and corrects the error and the group proceeds.

The Teacher's Role in Peer Control

The teacher is manager of the Peer Control Groups, procedure and materials. As manager, the teacher assigns students to groups, introduces oral reading skills, assigns reading passages, serves as a model for peer control, acts as consultant to the groups, and provides reinforcement.

10

Evidence of Effectiveness

The Cross-Cultural Approach is a multi-disciplinary strategy for teaching reading. It draws upon a number of disciplines, especially research in the area of linguistics (socio-linguistics) and psychology (learning and cognitive theory, among others). Embodied in this approach is what Rickford (1999) labeled "using the vernacular to teach the standard." Introducing students to reading in the vernacular and then switching them to reading in the standard is not new. Rickford states "this follows a principle that was established from research dating back to the 1950's. He cites Cheaver's (1957) dissertation on the use of vernacular language in education, where he reviewed studies around the world that indicated the effectiveness of using the vernacular to teach the standard.

Rickford also cites a study done in fourteen schools in the Philippines between 1948 and 1954 (Orto, 1953). In this study students who began instruction in the vernacular and later switched to the standard, "...very rapidly caught up with the students who started in English, and even surpassed them. These students outperformed students who started in English, in subjects ranging from reading to social studies and even arithmetic."

In Steward's (1969) research on the "development of special literacy programs designed to teach beginning reading in their vernacular language," cites a Swedish dialect study.

"Tore Osterberg found that the teaching of basic reading skills in the non-standard dialect of the school children in a particular district (Pitea) increased proficiency, not only in beginning reading in the non-standard dialect, but also in later reading in the standard language."

Baratz (1969), compared a group of White children residing in low to middle income communities with a group of Black inner-city children. The students in the 3rd and 5th grades were given a sentence repetition test consisting of 30 sentences, 15 in African American Language and 15 in Standard English. Baratz concluded from the research that, "there are two dialects involved in the education complex of Black children...Black children are generally not bi-dialectal and there is evidence of interferences from their dialect when Black children attempt to use Standard English."

Leaverton (1973) reported on the use of dialect reading materials as a basal reading program. In this study he used everyday talk (AAL) and school talk (SE) versions of four stories. The study focused on verb usage. He developed dialect readings which use 'everyday talk' and 'school talk'. The use of the verb 'got' for everyday talk and 'have' for school talk, were used in the readings. For example, 'I got' the ball and 'I have' the ball.

The stories were developed by recording conversations of kindergarten, first, second and third grade children in Chicago inner-city schools.

> Stop that!
> When I be talking, my teacher say 'stop that.'
> When I be running my teacher say, 'stop that.'
> When I be fighting, my teacher say, 'stop that.'

No talking
No running
No fighting
What a school

The 37 students were randomly placed in the SE control or experimental AAL groups by IQ scores. The experimental group received everyday talk stories and the control group received school talk stories.

Students in the experimental AAL group, with the help of the teacher, mastered the everyday talk stories and were tested for word and phrase recognition. The experimental AAL group then mastered the school talk stories and took a similar test. Leaverton wanted to ascertain whether the students learn to read everyday talk stories quicker than the school talk stories and if learning to read everyday talk stories aided in the learning of school talk stories. Leaverton reported results which were positive in favor of the experimental AAL group. Unfortunately the small number of students and lack of controls make it difficult to generalize his findings.

Hall, et al. (1979) conducted a similar experiment. They tested sixteen Black and White children in Headstart in New York City. They reported results which indicated that the Black children did considerably better on a story recall task when the story was presented in AAL. As in the case with Leaverton, the number of participants was not sufficiently large enough to generalize.

Williams and Rivers (1975) tested 900 Black children in kindergarten, first, and second grades on an Ebonics (AAL) version of the Boehm test of basic concepts. They hypothesized that Black children are not deficient due to their language in developing basic concepts; they simply represent these events differently. For example, if Black children have not associated *the word behind an object located spatially in back of another object*, the children are penalized on the test. If the children were asked where the object was, they would answer "in back of" making it clear that they have both the cognition and linguistic representation for that particular test item. William and Rivers reported that the children did considerably better on the Ebonics version of the test then on the original Standard English version.

Rickford (2000) reported that four of his students tested the response of twenty junior high school students in East Palo Alto (Maroney, et al., 1994) to dialect and Standard English versions of stories from the Bridge Reading Program. "Although the students were able to understand concepts from both stories, there was a higher frequency of correct answers for the AAL versions of the stories: *Dreamy Mae*—95.8 correct in AAL, versus 79.2% in SE; *A Friend in Need* —93.8% correct in AAL, versus 71.9% in SE."

However, Rickford and his wife, Angela, were unable to replicate the results. Rickford suggested that this was possibly due to lack of controls and small number of participants.

The Cultural Context of Cognition

An early study in a similar mode as Rickford, et al, was conducted by Charlsetta Simpkins Stalling (1976). This study was experimentally sound with an adequate number of participants, randomization, and other controls. With the invaluable assistance of Geneva Smitherman, Stalling was able to obtain access to Black students attending public schools in the Detroit area. I served as a consultant for the experimental design and analysis.

Three hundred and thirty four students in the seventh and eight grades attending predominantly Black schools in Detroit participated in the study. The subjects attended three schools which had an average enrollment of 85% Black students.

Eight classrooms were administered an assessment instrument entitled the 'Simpkins Test of Cultural Context' (STCC). The STCC was developed to assess the effects of the cultural context of language on the performance of students on a cognitive task. There are two forms in the STCC, Form A and Form B. Each Form is comprised of two subtests, *Meaning from Context* and *Figurative Language*. Each subtest contains a mini-lesson explanation on meaning from context and understanding figurative language. The mini-lessons are followed by fourteen test items in Standard English on each topic. There are two sections for each form; section one consists of a mini-lesson in Standard English and section two consists of a mini-lesson in African American Language.

On the two tasks, test items are held constant in Standard English while the mini-lessons explanations vary. The language used in the mini-lessons, Standard English and African American Language, reflect the language used in public school systems instructional materials (SE) and the language spoken by many inner city youth (AAL).

The STCC was administered to each regular classroom by its respective teacher. Using a table of random numbers, Forms A and B were placed in random order and distributed from left to right to the students. The teacher read aloud the standardized set of Teacher Directions. According to the directions the test timing is done by the teacher using the classroom wall clock. Upon completion of the test and at the end of the designated time allowed for taking the test, the tests were collected and taken to the main office of the school. The tests were then scored by a person who was unaware of the purpose of the test or the study.

One-way analysis of variance was used in the study. The independent variable was the instructional language used (AAL or SE). The students performance as measured by scores on the subtest of STCC served as the dependent variable. The results of the study were based on a sample of 234 seventh and eighth grade students attending three urban schools in the Detroit public school system.

Two one-way analyses of variance were performed on data from the total sample and each of the three schools: the subtest score on the *Meaning From Context* and *Figurative Language* tasks.

When the explanations were given in Standard English on the *Meaning from Context* subtest, the students obtained a mean score of 10.195 as compared to a mean score of 11.613 when the explanations were given in African American Language. The difference, 1.418, was highly significant (p<.001).

When explanations were given in Standard English for the *Figurative Language* subtest, the mean score of 5.585 compared to the mean score of 5.515 when explanations were given in African American Language. The difference, .960 was significant (p=.012).

Stalling reported that, "The overall results of the research supports the general hypothesis that when Black non-mainstream students are tested for their comprehension of reading materials in Standard English, they will do significantly better when the instructions for the reading materials are presented in African American Language, then when the instructions are presented in Standard English."

She went on to say, "in sum, the overall results of the study tend to support Simpkins' (1976) contention that the cognition of Black non-mainstream students is differentially affected by the cultural context of the language used in presenting and explaining a learning task…Simpkins postulated that differences in academic performance between Black non-mainstream students and mainstream students occur because the cognition apparatus of Black non-mainstream students is often differentially triggered by the cultural context of the language used."

Stalling stated that the results of her study were consistent with those of Williams and Rivers (1975) in their study of Black students on the Boehm test of Basic Concepts. She cites Williams and Rivers conclusion that; "...Black children are penalized by instructions on group tests which are presented in Standard English." The results of her studies were also similar to those reported by Stephen and John Baratz (1970) on a sentence repetition task.

Evaluating the Evolution of the Bridge Program

The program model for the Cross-Cultural Approach underwent a series of three evaluations. After each evaluation the program was further developed. These evaluations the original Los Angeles study, the Boston study and the Houghton Mifflin National Field Test.

Los Angeles Study

The purpose of this exploratory, preliminary evaluation (Simpkins 1969), was to gain some ideas of the integration, student response and effectiveness of various components of a African American Language (AAL) reading package under simulated classroom conditions. The evaluation was designed as a one group, pre-test/post-test experiment. Knowledge of reading was assessed before and after exposure to the reading materials. The study was conducted at California State University, Los Angeles under the auspices of the Secondary Education Department and the Associate Reading Clinic.

Eight Black inner-city high school dropouts, who were enrolled in the Neighborhood Youth Corp. out-of-school programs, were suddenly made available to participate in the study. Reading measures were obtained before and after exposure to the reading package using the California Reading Achievement test, Form W and Form X.

The staff consisted of one teacher, one aide, and an observer (located outside the classroom behind a one-way mirror). The staff was composed of Black undergraduates with no previous testing experience. The staff underwent a training session conducted by myself.

The AAL reading package was administered to the subjects two hours a day, four days a week, for six weeks. The class was taught by a teacher and an aide. An observer watched through the one-way mirror. I also observed the class. The aide and the observer exchanged roles every week.

The changes observed in the attitudes of the subjects toward reading were dramatic. The subjects regularly attended the classes and reported that "for the first time they felt that they were learning." They expressed a strong interest in attending the classes beyond the six weeks. They began reading other books and reading materials outside the class for the first time in their lives. They also reported that for the first time they enjoyed school and academic activities.

While the study was of a preliminary and exploratory nature, it provided me an opportunity to observe students representative of the target population interacting with the AAL reading package. No conclusions beyond these impressions could be drawn from the study. However, three principal recommendations emerged:

a) Offensive vernacular should be eliminated from the reading materials.

b) Additional material should be developed.

c) Future research should be conducted with greater controls, larger numbers of subjects, and a more sophisticated design and analysis of data.

The Boston Study

Based on insights gained from the Los Angeles study and additional research on reading, Black Dialect, and learning theory, the AAL reading package was remodeled and then evaluated in Boston (Simpkins, 1973). The evaluation included a control group and was designed as a pre-test/post-test, treatment (experimental) group/non-treatment (control) group experiment. Knowledge of reading was assessed before and after exposure or non-exposure to the AAL reading program.

The study was conducted at the Roxbury Boys Club in a Black inner-city area of Boston. Thirty Black inner-city students in the high school and junior high school age range, who resided in an urban inner-city area, participated in the study. A minimum reading level of grade 2.0 was set as a reading criteria for all subjects. The subjects also had to be at least one year behind the norm (grade level) in their scores.

Fifteen subjects were assigned to the treatment group and fifteen to the non-treatment control group. The groups were matched on IQ, age, and grade level. Neither group received additional reading instruction at school. Measures on the Nelson Reading Test and the Gray Oral Reading Test were obtained before and after exposure to the reading program. The Closson Intelligence Test was administered to all subjects for matching purposes.

The staff for the treatment group consisted of one teacher, one aide and one observer. The teacher was a graduate student in education. The aide and observer were members of the Boys Club staff. Both the aide and observer had an undergraduate background. The staff underwent a training program conducted by myself.

The AAL reading program was administered to the treatment group for five hours per week (Monday 1.5 hours, Tuesday 1.5 hours, and Wednesday 2 hours) for twelve weeks. The teachers taught the class assisted by the aide. The aide and the observer exchanged roles every two weeks.

Four analyses of covariance were performed on the post-test scores for the following measures; (a) the vocabulary subtest of the Nelson Reading Test; (b) the comprehension subtest of the Nelson reading Test; (c) the total score for the Nelson Reading Test; (d) and the Gray Oral Reading test. The factors in each analysis were sex and group (treatment/non-treatment). The covariates in each analysis were age and pre-test score on the same measures.

Mean pre-test scores for the four reading measures (expressed in grade equivalences), ages in months, grade and IQ's are presented in Table 10.1. Scores are presented for the experimental and control groups with each group broken down by sex.

The means for the subtests in each group indicate that the experimental AAL group students scored higher than the control group on all reading measures.

There were no significant differences by sex on any of the four reading measures. Significant differences between the AAL dialect groups were obtained on three of the four reading measures. When post-test scores were adjusted for age and pre-test levels, the experimental AAL group scored significantly higher than the control group on the Nelson Comprehension subtest, ($p<.01$); Nelson total score, ($p=.03$); and the Gray Oral Reading test, ($p<.001$). Although the experimental AAL groups score on the Nelson Vocabulary subtest failed to reach significance, ($p>.05$), the difference was in the predicted direction ($p=.07$).

For those who would like all this in plain English, the following might help. The statistical level of significance addresses the probability that the results of an experiment occurred by real change instead of chance. For this study, a .05 level of significance was set. This means that there are five chances in a hundred that the results occurred by chance. If p is less than .05 (p<.05) then we say that we have significance at the .05 level. If p is more than .05 (p>.05) then we say the data did not reach significance. If p is close to .05, for example p=.07, then we say that the p or the difference for the measurement was in the predicted direction.

The reader should keep in mind that the smaller the sample size, the harder it is to reach significance. While a gain of 2 months

Table 10.1

Mean IQ's and Mean Grade Equivalent Pre-test Scores on Four Reading Measures

Measure	Experimental			Control		
	Males	Females	Total	Males	Females	Total
Nelson Vocabulary	5.16	3.22	4.35	6.35	5.10	6.10
Nelson Comprehension	4.14	1.56	3.07	4.55	3.15	4.27
Nelson Total	4.66	2.78	3.87	5.51	4.50	5.31
Gray Oral	4.67	3.10	4.61	4.05	5.51	3.98
Age in Months	171.29	153.60	163.91	177.00	177.00	175.00
Grade	3.00	6.40	7.33	7.57	7.57	7.66
IQ	87.57	86.00	86.83	86.25	86.50	86.30
N	7	5	12	8	2	10

might be significant with a sample size of 300, a gain of 12 months may not be with a sample size of 12.

The experimental AAL group had a mean total gain score on the Nelson Reading test of 1.04 years as compared to a mean open score of 0.06 years for the control group. On the Gray Oral Reading test, the AAL experimental AAL group had a mean gain score of 1.32 years as compared to a mean gain score of 0.18 years for the control group.

As in the Los Angeles study, the students were eager to attend and showed dramatic changes in their attitude toward reading. Toward the end of the study, the students began requesting that the teacher recommend books for them to read that she enjoyed. After the first week, there were very few discipline problems. The students were on task about 85 to 90% of the time.

The results from the evaluation were extremely promising. They seemed to indicate that the reading program had the potential for becoming an effective tool for teaching reading to Black inner-city youth. Although the data was encouraging, I expressed reservations. I would have liked to have had a much larger sample size and more controls. Although this study provided valuable insights, I felt that there was a need for further development and research.

Houghton Mifflin National Field Test

When Houghton Mifflin Publishing Company approached me, I refused to allow them to release the Bridge Reading Program unless it was evaluated and the evaluation showed strong evidence of effectiveness. One of the Vice Presidents of Houghton Mifflin told me that evaluation was a waste of time and money due to the fact that school districts do not purchase programs based on evaluation data.

He went on to relate a story about a certain math program which the company tested and found to be highly effective in teaching students math. The company also had a program which left a great deal to be desired in terms of teaching math. Despite the impressive data on the math program, it was a financial disaster. The school districts failed to purchase the program, while on the other hand the program which was very weak became one of their all time best sellers due to its cosmetic features. However, despite their reservations regarding *Bridge*, the company agreed to conduct an extensive evaluation as I requested.

In 1975, an experimental edition of *Bridge: A Cross Cultural Reading Program* (Simpkins, et al., 1974) was field tested in school systems in various areas of the United States. The field test was designed by Houghton Mifflin Publishing and myself, to test the *Bridge Reading Program* under actual, day to day classroom conditions.

The school systems were approached by the publishing company and asked to use their remedial reading program, already planned for the upcoming semester, as a control group. This was done in order to compare *Bridge* with the normal remedial reading activities of the schools.

The evaluation was designed as an Experimental AAL group, Control Group, Pre-test, Post-test experiment. Knowledge of reading was assessed before and after exposure to the reading activities of both groups. The five field centers were located in school systems in Chicago, Illinois; Phoenix, Arizona; Washington, D.C.; Memphis, Tennessee; and Macon County Alabama.

Five hundred and forty students enrolled in 27 classes at the high school and junior high school levels participated as subjects in the study. Of the 540 students 530 were Black. Fourteen teachers were selected by the schools to participate in the field test. The same teacher taught both the experimental and control group classes. The *Bridge Program* and the previously planned remedial reading activities were administered to students for a period of time equivalent to one class room hour, 5 days a week for four months.

Reading measures were obtained before and after exposure to the *Bridge Program* and the control group's previously planned reading programs, using the Iowa Test of Basic Skills in Reading Comprehension level 12 forms. With the publishing company, I developed a field test questionnaire to assess the students and teachers response to various components of the *Bridge Program*.

The experimental AAL group and the control group (students given previously planned remedial reading activities) displayed very different levels of gain scores at the end of the program. The experimental AAL group displayed a mean gain in grade equivalency scores of 6.2 months for 4.0 months of instruction. The control group displayed a mean gain of 1.6 months for 4.0 months of instruction. At the seventh grade level, the experimental AAL group has a mean gain of 4.9 months for 4.0 months of instruction, as compared to a mean gain of 2.8 months for the control group. At the eighth grade level, the experimental AAL group had a mean gain of 9.3 months for 4.0 months of instruction as compared to a mean gain of 3.5 months for the control group. At the ninth through twelfth grade level, the experimental AAL group had a mean gain of 5.2 months for 4.0 months instruction, compared to a mean loss of 4.9 months for the control group.

At each of the grade levels, the experimental AAL group students had a mean gain score in excess of the normative level; namely, 4.0 months of instruction. The control group students had a mean gain score below the normative level at each of the grade levels.

A statistical test performed on the data indicated that the differences between the experimental and control groups for the total sample (grades 7-12) were highly significant ($p < .005$). There were also significant differences between the experimental and control groups at the eighth grade level (p<.02) and at the ninth grade level (p,.001).

The results of the Teacher Questionnaire indicated that the students found the *Bridge Program* highly enjoyable and easy to follow and understand. Students were able to proceed independently through the structured sequence after approximately one or two weeks. The teachers consistently reported that the behavior management section was extremely effective in keeping students on task and that they experienced fewer discipline problems in the classroom.

Students exhibited high motivational levels throughout the program. All teachers reported that students enjoyed working with the program "and were motivated to do well." The following are representative teacher comments: "All students enjoy working with *Bridge*"; "students have developed a positive attitude toward *Bridge*; "Students never complain and are eager to read."; "Students are anxious to begin to work."; "Low achievers are interested in this program."; "Even my chronic troublemakers are willing to listen to direction and remain on task."; "The test may or may not prove that a lot has been gained, but one thing is for certain: students attitudes toward reading have changed."

All teachers reported that the content of the stories interested the students. Some of their comments were: "They like the stories because they are able to read them."; "The objective to create an interest in the reading material was accomplished."; "Students are enjoying the program."; "The stories reminded students of their families."

Reactions were mixed concerning the use of three versions of the same stories and their effect on student interest. Most teachers indicated that student interest was sustained while reading African American Language, Transition and Standard English versions of the same story. Other teachers felt that the three versions of the same story were unnecessary. Teachers reported that Story Questions scores went up while students were working on stories with extra versions.

Most teachers reported that students would not enjoy the program without the African American Language stories. However, students remained interested in the Unit V (step 5) materials even though they were in Standard English.

According to the teachers, students could follow the directions given for answering the Story Questions. Data from the teachers indicated that the average of correct answers for the Story Questions was seven out of ten in Unit I (Step 1), but by Unit V (Step 5), the average of correct answers was nine out of ten.

Most teachers reported that students were able to carry out Peer Control procedures with help from the teachers in getting started. Students had no difficulty in reading or understanding the stories. The reading groups were orderly and the different methods of choosing the order of Readers did not present any problems in most classes. The students enjoyed Peer Control Reading. The teachers' data indicated that students remained interested while reading two and three versions of the same story.

Teachers wanted more Peer Control stories. They believed that students improved their reading through Peer Control. The following are representative teacher comments on Peer Control: "Peer Control Reading makes students realize how much they need practice in reading."; "This activity made everyone read."; "The students became mistake conscious and tried to pronounce the words better."; "Students look forward to Peer Control and often hate to stop when the bell rings." Most teachers reported that students enjoyed keeping records of their own scores but often needed teacher assistance.

The questionnaires indicate that teacher attitudes toward the program and Black dialect improved as the students proceeded through the materials. Several teachers, at the beginning of the program, reported what appeared to be negative perceptions of the program and Black dialect, but were writing glowing reports toward the end of the program.

From an experimental point of view, the field test, as is the case in most field tests performed by publishing companies, left much to be desired. The teachers and the students were assigned to experimental and control groups by the school rather than on a random basis. Students in the experimental AAL group had lower pre-test scores than the control group students. It appears that, although the teachers denied it, the schools tended to place the students whom they considered most in need of help in the experimental AAL groups. This practice suggested the possibility of regression effects. There is also the possibility of the "Hawthorne Effect" due to the novelty of the program and the use of Black dialect. However, it must be understood that this evaluation was done in the natural environment, not in the laboratory.

My contract stipulated that the program would not be marketed unless both the publishers and I jointly agreed that there were clear indications from the field test that the program was effective in teaching Black students to improve their reading performance. This stipulation insured that the program would not be marketed for "cosmetic features" alone. The results of the field test were extremely encouraging to me, my co-authors and the publishers.

Directions for Future Research and Development

There is a need for further experimentation with the Cross-Cultural Approach to Reading. Future studies should be of both an experimental and field test nature. Measures should be taken of attitudinal variables such as sense of control of the environment, student motivational levels and interest in reading.

Behavioral measures such as time on task should also be taken. It would be interesting to ascertain the amount of test variance the Peer Control Procedure accounted for and there exists a great need to develop material for students in the elementary levels. Another great need is for long term studies to ascertain whether or not the gain lasts across time and is generalized to other subjects.

Since the publication of the results of the Houghton Mifflin Field test on *Bridge* (Simpkins and Simpkins, 1974), which have been cited by numerous linguists, I, despite an extensive review of the literature, know of no large scale research, or for that matter any medium scale research, using the difference model on reading or any other subjects. Although none dares call it racism, I firmly believe the stereotyped concepts of African American Language embraced by government and foundation research money brokers has a great deal to do with the poverty of funding for research and development in this area.

As mentioned in the opening chapter, the Black non-mainstream student is literally between a rock (the simulative dialect) and a hard place (the government and the educational establishments plans to implement standardized testing for retention promotion). I hope this book will enlighten governmental and educational policy makers to the fact that there are many roads which lead to Rome and it is not always desirable to take the royal road.

11

Concluding

Remarks

The Bush Administration has enacted the most sweeping changes in educational policy in over three decades. The legislation, which is intended to reduce the academic achievement gap between haves and have nots, mainstream and non-mainstream students in this country's public school system, represents an extremely ambitious attempt at educational reform. It has been described as Bush's "accountability" policy for the schools.

In the past the federal government's educational reform efforts have focused on eliminating the inequality of educational resources. The new government reform efforts represent a rewrite and redirection of the 1965 Elementary and Secondary Education Act. The new law requires every state to select, design, and administer tests in grades three through eight by the 2005–2006 school year. Students will be required to take annual reading and math tests. It is the intent of the federal government to establish a national set of standards in order to ensure that all students are mastering basic reading skills in the reading and math areas with science to be added at a later date.

All states will be required to test sample groups of fourth and eighth graders. These test scores will be compared against a national achievement test entitled the National Assessment of Educational Progress (NAEP). School districts will be required to submit to the public and the government annual reports that compare their schools' standardized test scores and teacher qualifications with those of other schools on the state and national level. Exit exam results and high school graduation rates will be included in the reports. The data will be broken down by race, gender and socio-economic status. The reports are intended to assist parents in determining which schools are making the most progress at closing the achievement gap.

Schools that show little or no improvement will receive additional funds to improve their programs. If a school fails to improve deficient test scores for two consecutive years students may transfer to another school. If a school fails to make progress in three years it will be required to offer tutorial services. After four years, the state is required to take punitive measures, such as replacing staff and curriculum. The Bush Administration intended the bill to include vouchers for children attending schools which fail to improve, but was forced to back away from the voucher plan in order to appease conservatives and to achieve a bipartisan consensus.

The Bush educational reform program is a reaction to the failure of the nations public schools to close the achievement gap between mainstream and non-mainstream students. It also reflects group frustration with the public schools' inability to adequately prepare students to take their place in a high-tech global economy due to lack of basic academic skills. It is a reaction against years of acceptance of failure by the schools, and the reality that our public school system does not measure up when compared to those of European countries and Japan.

But unless the Bush Administration can break the grip of the cumulative deficit on Black non-mainstream students, it cannot claim success for its school reform efforts. The battle cry of the Bush Administration, "no child will be left behind" could very well come back to haunt it in a similar manner as "read my lips" did for the "no new taxes" pledge of the senior Bush. There are no short term, get tough accountability solutions for non-mainstream schools. Unfortunately the problem is more complex. While Bush is to be applauded for attempting to document the academic achievement problem of this country's public school system, he has, in many ways, unknowingly opened a Pandora's box.

If educational reform efforts are to be successful, they must benefit from the mistakes of the past. They must be aware of how the government's previous efforts at educational reform failed to help Black non-mainstream students close the achievement gap. It is one thing to document the scope of the problem and quite another to intervene with any degree of success.

When the data collected from testing in the individual states are analyzed, the government and the public will begin to comprehend the enormity of the problem. They will begin to discover that, far from realizing the well intended goal of President Bush's "no child will be left behind", hundreds of thousands of children in the past and present continue to be left behind.

The public schools, at this time, have no conceptual or theoretical framework for addressing the "cumulative deficit". The longer Black non-mainstream students remain in school, the farther behind they become in their achievements as compared to their White peers. Without a framework for addressing this problem, the schools will continue to do what they have done in the past with the same poor results.

The President would like to see schools use proven methods of instruction. The problem is there are very few proven methods of instruction for Black non-mainstream students. A twenty percent increase in federal funding is only the beginning. The federal government has just entered step one of a cycle that will require more and more funding with fewer and fewer returns.

Once the impact of the bill's testing requirement is felt, the increased dropout rate and lower graduation rate of Black students from high school will be a source of national embarrassment and alarm. Many high school principals are already losing sleep over the numbers of Black students who will not graduate due to failure to pass the high school exit exam. In numerous inner city high schools, 20 to 40% of the senior class are failing to pass these exams. Currently, an ever increasing amount of school time is being devoted to practicing for the exams. In the future look for even more school time to be used on studying for the test as opposed to studying subject matter.

The new Bush legislation appears to believe that tutoring and punitive measures for the schools will solve the problem: that Black non-mainstream students will learn what they have failed to learn in the past, basic skills in reading and math. The new legislation does not really address the learning problems of the public school throwaways.

Many are of the opinion that we may have to face the reality of writing off older students in the system and focus resources on the K–3 level. A great many educators are also of the opinion that we need to start over with an emphasis on the elementary grade levels. California, in an effort to raise the educational achievement level of its school systems chose to intervene at the K–3 level. The state poured billions of dollars into the schools in an effort to reduce the pupil teacher classroom ratio. While the program was successful in lowering the teacher-student ratio at the K–3 level (and this is an ongoing process), the latest evaluation of academic achievement showed no significant difference. After billions of dollars, no significant difference!

The President and the public schools are in need of help. The kind of help that only social science-based research can provide. Over the past three decades, the public school system has proven itself to be incapable of addressing the cumulative deficit of Black non-mainstreamed students in regard to their reading performance.

The approach of using these students' African American Language derived from their social environments in the street, provides one such approach that has demonstrated considerable promise. This approach strongly motivated the most difficult of these students who have suffered many years of failure in learning to read—the hardest core population to reach. It motivated them to read, got them excited and goal oriented. They worked at the reading task in focussed ways that teachers who had worked with them in the past had not seen them do before. They took responsibility for their reading within the social environment to which they were accustomed—working with their peers. Teachers assumed roles that oriented them to the next task and provided support as they went through the tasks. Given this positive context for the reading, they made a six month gain in only four months of work, more than triple the gain of the students working in the standard program.

Several factors which are not typical for these students must be emphasized: their strong motivation and interest in the reading materials, the disappearance of acting-out behavioral problems that invariably characterize these classrooms, and the desire that was ignited to continue reading books the teachers suggested. The dominant atmosphere—very positive, goal oriented and motivated—is reflected in the improved scores following the intervention. One can only ignore the students' response to such programs for ideological reasons—and at peril to these students' future academic performance!

This program is one example of how social science based research can be mobilized to provide direction for the schools' intervention plans using proven evaluation methodologies. It is time to apply what was learned from the errors of the sixties so that truly "no child will be left behind".

Appendix

Bridge Talk

by Merrill Sheils with Richard Manning in Boston
Newsweek, December 20, 1976

Now check this out. Quiet as it's kept, you do need this here reading program. If you sitting in this class, you don't be readin' any too cool. Now don't be lookin' around. I'm talkin' about you. Here, right over there. Right over there in the corner. Unless you the teacher, I'm talkin' about you.

The voice on the tape is smooth, silky, its accents and idioms easy on the streetwise ear—and in many inner-city schools, it may soon sound as familiar as the voice of the English teacher. The tape is included in a new black-studies system called "Bridge: A Cross-Culture Reading Program." It is a reading course aimed at black teen-agers who read at levels far below the norms for their age. Based on John Dewey's axiom that effective education must "start where the child is," Bridge uses the vernacular black youngsters hear and speak at home to move them toward proficiency in standard English.

Bridge, which will be published next month by Houghton Mifflin, is the brainchild of Gary Simpkins, 33, an assistant professor of special education at Westfield (Mass.) State College. As a teacher for Head Start and the Job Corps in the 1960s, Simpkins found that many able black youngsters had to struggle so hard to bridge the gap between their everyday speech and standard English that they simply gave up in desperation. "They have a sophisticated oral culture of their own," says Simpkins. "They're not dumb—you just have to get to them in their own environment."

'Superbad Ship': That is precisely what Bridge is designed to do. With his wife, Charlesetta, who works for the Massachusetts Department of Education, and Grace Holt, professor of speech and director of black studies at the University of Illinois, Chicago Circle, Simpkins has compiled a five-booklet system that teaches kids by building on the language they already use. The program starts with stories in black vernacular. "Shine," the first entry, is about a black stoker on the Titanic—"the biggest and baddest ship ever to sail the sea." The Titanic, the story reveals, was supposed to be unsinkable. "It was a superbad ship, the meanest thing on the water. It could move like four bloods in tennis shoes."

In the exercises that accompany the story, students practice finding equivalents for the black vernacular phrases. Even the directions for the exercises are in dialect. (Sample: "Go for what you know about the story 'Shine' ...There ain't but one right answer to each question, so don't be picking out two.") There are subtle lessons in almost every exercise. For instance, in translating "it could move like four bloods in tennis shoes" to "it was a real fast ship," the students gain valuable insight into the construction and use of simile.

Proficiency: From vernacular, the program moves to a "transition form" of language that is somewhere between street and standard dialects, and then on to standard English itself. At midpoint in the course, students work with stories and exercises in all three forms. By the time they reach volume five, they are supposed to be proficient enough in standard English to work with that alone, although directions in vocabulary exercises encourage them to continue to draw on black vernacular phrases for richness and variety. "What we're saying," explains Charlesetta Simpkins, "is 'Hey, the way you speak is OK, but you're going to need another way, too, outside'."

Field tests of the Bridge program have been extremely promising. In the spring of 1975, 540 students from Chicago, Washington, Phoenix, Memphis and Macon County, Ala., were tested for reading proficiency. Then 417 worked with Bridge, while the others kept at a standard curriculum. The Bridge students gained 6.2 months in reading achievement over the four-month experiment. The control group gained only 1.6.

Some black educators are not convinced that Simpkins's "cross-cultural" approach is a good idea. Psychologist Kenneth Clark, for example, has long argued that soul talk has no place in a curriculum, and thinks that black youngsters should have rigorous training in the traditional disciplines of standard English. But the designers of Bridge emphasize that their program is aimed specifically at inner-city teen-agers who have already failed to respond to such methods. By starting afresh, and working from the language they are most comfortable with, Simpkins thinks, many of them find, to their surprise, that reading all kinds of English is a skill they can master—and enjoy. Bridge, its promoters hope, may give these youngsters a precious second chance.

References

Alexander, K.L. Entwesle, D.R., & Dauhe, S.L. (1994). *On the success of failure: A reassessment of the effect of retention in the primary grades.* Cambridge, England: Cambridge Univ. Press.

Altschuler, A.S. (1973) Promoting human development through psychological education. *Models and Strategies.* Boston: Training and Development Systems.

Anderson, D.K. (1994). *Paths through secondary education: Race/ethnic and gender differences.* Unpublished doctoral dissertation. University of Wisconsin-Madison.

Bailey, B. (1965). Linguistics and non-standard language patterns. Paper presented to the National Council of Teachers of English.

Bailey, B. (1968). Some aspects of the impact of linguistics on teaching in disadvantaged communities. *Elementary English, 45.*

Baratz, J. (1968). Language development in he economically disadvantaged child. *American Speech and Hearing Association, 10,* 143-145.

Baratz, J. (1969). Teaching reading in an urban negro school system. In J. Baratz & Shuey, R. (Eds.), *Teaching black children to read.* Washington, D.C.: Center for Applied Linguistics.

Baratz, J. (1973). Language abilities of black americans-review of research: 1966-1970. Unpublished paper, Education Study Center, Washington, D.C.

Baratz, S. & Baratz, J. (1970, Winter). Early childhood intervention: the social base of institutional racism. *Harvard Education Review, 40.*

Barnes, E.J. (1972). Cultural retardation or shortcomings of assessment techniques? In R.L. Jones (Ed.), *Black Psychology.* New York: Harper and Row.

Barnes, E.J. (1974). The utilization of behavior and social sciences in minority group education. In E. Epps (Ed.), *Cultural pluralism.* Philadelphia: McCuthcan Publishing Corp.

Bereiter, C. (1965). Academic instruction and preschool children. In R. Cobin and M. Crosby (Eds.), *Language programs for the disadvantaged.* Champaign, Illinois: National Council of Teachers of English.

Bereiter, C. & Engelmann, S. (1962). *Language learning activities for the disadvantaged child.* (ERIC Document Reproduction Service No. Ed 020 002).

Bereiter, C. & Engelmann, S. (1966). *Teaching disadvantaged children in the pre-school.* Englewood Cliffs, N.J.: Prentice-Hall.

Bloom, B.J., et al. (1965). *Compensatory education for cultural deprivation.* New York: Holt.

Budoff, M. (1969). Learning potential: a supplementary procedure for assessing the ability to reason. *Seminars in Psychiatry, 1.*

Cazden, C. (1967). Individual differences in language competence. *Journal of Special Education, 2.*

Cazden, C. Baratz, J., Labov, W. & Palmer, F. (1970). *State of the art.* Washington, D.C.: U.S. Office of Economic Opportunity.

Clark, A. & Richards, C. (1966). Auditory discrimination among economically disadvantaged and non-disadvantaged preschool children. *Exceptional Children, 33,* 259-62.

Clark, K.B. (1968). Alternative public school systems. *Harvard Educational Review, 38,* 100-113.

Clinton, W.J. (1998). *Memorandum to the secretary of education.* White House press release, Washington, D.C.

Cole, M., Gay, J., Glick, J. & Sharp, D. (1971). *The cultural context of learning and thinking: an exploration in experimental anthropology.* New York: Basic Books, Inc.

Coleman, J., Campbell, E.G., Hobson, C.J., McPartland, J., Mood, A.M., Weinfeld, F.B. & York, R.L. (1966). *Equality of educational opportunity.* U.S. Department of Health, Education, and Welfare. Washington, D.C.: U.S. Government Printing Office.

Corbin, R. & Crosby, M. (1965). *Language programs for the disadvantaged.* Champaign, Illinois: National Council of Teachers of English.

Covington, A. (1975). Teacher attitude toward black English. In R.L. Williams (Ed.), *Ebonics: the true language of black folks.* St. Louis: The Institute of Black Studies.

Cronbach, L.J. (1970). *Essentials of psychological testing.* New York: Harper and Row.

Day, N.A. (1968). Organization for social and technical innovation. *Harvard Educational Review, 38,* 133-143.

DeStefano, J. (1973). Black English. In Johanna DeStefano (Ed.), *Language, society, and education: a profile of black english.* Worthington, Ohio: Charles A. Jones Publishing Company.

Deutsch, C. (1964). Auditory discrimination and learning social factors. *Merrill-Palmer Quarterly, 10*, 277-296.

Deutsch, M. (1960). Minority group and class status as related to social and personality factors in scholastic achievement. *Monograph of the Society for Applied Anthropology*, no. 1. Ithaca, New York: Cornell University Press.

Deutsch, M. (1963). The disadvantaged child and learning process. In Passow (Ed.), *Education in depressed areas*. New York: Columbia University, Teachers College.

Deutsch, M. (1965). The role of social class in language development and cognition. *American Journal of Orthopsychiatry, 35*.

Deutsch, M. & Brown, B. (1964). Social influences in negro-white intelligence differences. *Journal of Social Issues, 20*.

Deutsch et al. (1967). *The disadvantaged child*. New York: Basic Books.

Dickeman, M. (1973). Teaching cultural pluralism. In J.A. Banks (Ed.) *Teaching Ethnic Studies* (43rd Yearbook). Washington, D.C.: National Council for the Social Studies.

Dillard, J.L. (1972). *Black English*. New York: Random House.

Dillard, J.L. (1967). Negro children's dialect in the inner city. *Florida FL Reporter, 5*, No. 3.

Dillard, J.L. (1966). The urban language study of the center for applied linguistics. *Florida FL Reporter*, 1-2.

Engelmann, S. (1967). *The basic concept inventory*. Chicago: Follett Publishing Co.

Erickson, E., Bryan, C. & Walker, L. (1972, January). The educability of dominant groups. *Phi Delta Kappen*.

Erickson, E. & Krumbein, E. (1971, Summer). Ecology and education: and open system model for urban independent schools. *Journal of Research and Development in Education, 4*.

Garcia, S., Blackwell, A., Williams, C. & Simpkins, G.A. (1969). *Research in the black community: a need for self-determinism*. Southwest Regional Laboratory, U.S. Office of Education, October.

Garrett, H.E. (1961). The equalitarian dogma. *Mankind Quarterly, 1*.

Glaser, R. (1972). Individuals and learning: the new attitude. *Educational Researcher, 1*.

Glazer, N. & Moynihan, D. (1963). *Beyond the melting pot*. Cambridge, Massachusetts: MIT Press and Harvard University Press.

Goldenberg, I. (1973). Direct revenue-sharing with the poor: an alternative model for future programs in the area of human and institutional renewal. In *Models and strategies*. Boston: Training and Development Systems.

Goodman, K. (1965, December). Dialect barriers to reading comprehension. *Elementary English*.

Green, R. (1964). Dialect sampling and language values. In R. Shuey (Ed.), *Social dialects and language learning*. Champaign, Illinois: National Council of Teachers of English.

Green, R. (1972). The black quest for higher education: an admission dilemma. In R. L. Jones (Ed.), *Black Psychology*. New York: Harper and Row.

Grier, W.H. & Cobbs, F.M. (1968). *Black rage*. New York: Basic Books.

Guilford, J.P. (1967). *The nature of human intelligence*. New York: McGraw Hill.

Gunnings, T. (1972). Psychological, *educational*, and economic effects of compensatory education programs on blacks. In R. L. Jones (Ed.), *Black Psychology*. New York: Harper and Row.

Hammond, R. & Simpkins, G.A. (1973). *Favorable learning environment through non-reactive discipline control*. Unpublished paper.

Harris, J.A. (1970). *How to increase reading ability*. New York: David McKay Company.

Herber, R. (1968). The influence of environment and genetic variables. In H. J., Prehm, L. A. Hemerlynch, and J. E. Crosson (Eds.), *Behavior research in mental retardation*. Eugene, Oregon Press.

Hess, R. & Shipman, V. (1985). Early experience and socialization of cognitive modes in children. *Child Development*, 6, 869-886.

Hess, R., Shipman, V., Brophy, J. & Bear, R. (1968). *The cognitive environment of urban preschool children*. The Graduate School of Education, The University of Chicago.

Hickey, T. (1973). Bilingualism and the measurement of intelligence and verbal learning ability. *Exceptional Children*, *39*.

Holmes, C.T. (1989). Grade level retention: A meta-analysis of research studies. In L.A. Shepard and M.L. Smith (Eds.), *Flunking grades: Research and policies on retention*. (pp.16-33) London: Falmer Press.

Holt, G. (1971). *Metaphor, black discourse style and cultural reality*. Unpublished paper presented at the Seventh Annual Southern Conference on Language Teaching, Atlanta.

House, E.R. (1989). Policy implications of retention research. In L.A. Shepard and M.L. Smith (Eds.), *Flunking grades: Research and policies on retention.* (pp.202-215). London: Falmer Press.

Humphreys, L. (1969). Letters. *Science, 66.*

Hunt, L. (1961). *Intelligence and experience.* New York: Ronald Press.

Hurst, C. (1965). *Psychological correlates in dialectolalia.* Washington, D.C.: Howard University, Communities Research Center.

Jensen, A. (1969). How much can we boost IQ and scholastic achievement? *Harvard Education Review, 39.*

Jensen, A. (1973, December). The differences are real. *Psychology Today.*

Johnson, K. R. (1970). *Teaching the culturally disadvantaged.* California: Science Research Associates, College Division.

Jones, A. (1960). *An investigation of the response patterns differentiating the performance of selected negro and white freshman on SCAT.* Unpublished doctoral dissertation, University of Colorado.

Kagan, J. (1973, July). *The IQ puzzle: what are we measuring?* Harvard University, Center for Law and Education, *43.*

Katz, L. (1967). The socialization of academic motivation in minority group children. *Nebraska Symposium on Motivation.* Lincoln: University of Nebraska Press.

Kennedy, W.A., Vernon, V. & White, J. (1963). A normative sample of intelligence and achievement of negro elementary school children in southeastern United States. *Monographs of the Society for Research in Child Development, 28*(b).

Kerlinger, F. (YEAR). *Foundations of behavioral research.* New York: Holt, Rinehart, and Winston.

Kochman, T. (1969, Spring/Summer). Culture and communication: implications for black english in the classroom. *The Florida FL Reporter.*

Kuhn, T. (1970). *The structure of scientific revolutions.* Chicago: The University of Chicago Press.

Labov, W. (1967). The non-standard vernacular of the negro community: some practical suggestions. *Seminar in English and Language Arts,* Temple University.

Labov, W. (1969). The logic of non-standard English. *Georgetown University Monographs,* Washington, D.C., No. 122.

Labov, W. & Cohen, P. (1967). Systematic relations of standard rule in grammar of negro speakers. *Project Literacy, 7.*

Labov, W. & Cohen, P., Robins, & Lewis, J. (1965). *A preliminary study of the structure of English used by negro and Puerto Rican speakers in New York City*. Cooperative Research Project, Columbia University.

Labov, W. & Cohen, P., Robins, Lewis, J. (1968). *A study of the non-standard English for negro and Puerto Rican speakers in New York City* Vols. 1 and 2. 6-10-059, Cooperative Research Project.

Larson, R. & Cloon, J. (1963). A method of identifying culturally disadvantaged kindergarten children. *Exceptional Children*.

Legum, S.E., Williams, C.E., & Lee, M.T. (1973). *Social dialects and their implications for school systems with high percentages of minority students*. (Vol. 2). The National Alliance of Black School Superintendents, Tuskegee, Alabama.

Lewis, M.H. et al. (1973). *Program research and development for school systems with high percentages of minority students*. Tuskegee, Alabama: The National Alliance of Black School Superintendents, *11*.

McClelland, D. (1968). *The achieving society*. Glencoe, Illinois: Free Press.

Montague, D.O. (1964). Arithmetic concepts of kindergarten children in contrasting socio-economic areas. *Elementary Schools, 64*.

Moore, D. (1968). *Competence and performance factors in the development of sentences in children of different social classes*. Unpublished paper, University of Illinois.

Moore, D. (1971). Language research in preschool language training. In C. S. Lavatelli (Ed.), *Language training in early childhood education*. Champaign, Illinois: University of Illinois Press.

Mosteller, F. and D. P. Moynihan, Eds. (1972). *On equality of educational opportunities*.

National Research Council. (1966). *High stakes: Testing for tracking, promotion and graduation*. Washington, D.C.: National Academy Press.

O'Neil, W. (1971). The politics of bidialecticalism. In Kampf & Lauter (Eds.), *The politics of literature*. New York: Pantheon.

Osborn, R.T. (1960). Racial differences in mental growth and school achievement: a longitudinal study. *Psychological Reports, 7*.

Prichard, J. (1851). *Researches into the physical history of man*. London.

Rickford, J.R. (1999). *African american vernacular English*. Cambridge, MA: Blackwell Publishers.

Rivers, L. (1969). *The stability of patterns of primary mental abilities in children from three different ethnic groups.* Unpublished doctoral dissertation, St. Louis University.

Roberts, E. (1970). *An evaluation of standardized tests as tools for the measurement of language development.* Unpublished paper, Language Research Foundation, Cambridge, MA.

Scholnick, E. K., Osler, S. F. & Kalzenellenbogen, R. (1968, March). Discrimination and concept identification in disadvantaged and middle class children. *Child Development, 39.*

Serage, H. (1973). The culturally deprived reader: research, diagnosis, and prescriptions. *The Library Quarterly.*

Shepard, L.A. & Smith, M.L. (1987). Effects of kindergarten retention at the end of first grade. *Psychology in the School.*

Shepard, L.A. (1991). A review of the research on kindergarten retention. In L.A. Shepard and M.L Smith (Eds.) *Thinking grades: Research and policy on retention.* (pp. 64-78). London: Falmer Press.

Sheils, M. & Manning, R. (1976, Dec. 20). Bridge talk. *Newsweek.*

Shuey, A. (1958). *The testing of negro intelligence.* Lynchburg, Virginia: Bell Press.

Silberman, H.F. (1965). Reading and related verbal learning. In R. Glass (Ed.), *Teaching machines and programmed learning* (Vol. 3). Washington, D.C.: National Educational Association of the United States.

Simpkins, C. & Simpkins, G.A. (1975). *Simpkins test of cultural context.* Unpublished test.

Simpkins, G.A. (1969). Initial evaluation: technomics reading and writing instructional package. Santa Monica, California: Technomics Research and Analysis Corp.

Simpkins, G.A. (1973, January). *Reading, black dialect and associative bridging.* Paper presented at the Conference on Cognitive and Language Development of the Black Child, National Institute of Health, St. Louis.

Simpkins, G.A. (1976). *Social science research on black non-mainstream children: the ugly American syndrome.* Unpublished paper.

Simpkins, G.A., Gunnings, T. (1972, October). The black six-hour retarded child. *Journal of Non-White Concerns.*

Simpkins, G.A., Holt, G. & Simpkins, C. (1971). *Bridge: a cross-culture reading program* (Experimental edition). Boston: Houghton Mifflin.

Simpkins, G.A., Smitherman, G., & Stalling, C. (2001). *Bridge 2: A cross-cultural reading program.* Cambridge, MA: Brookline Books.

Stanton, W. (1960). *The leopard's spots: scientific attitudes toward race in America.* Chicago: The University of Chicago Press.

Steward, W. (1967, Spring). Sociolinguistic factors in the history of American negro dialects. *The Florida FL Reporter, 5.*

Steward, W. (1968). Continuity and change in american negro dialects. *The Florida FL Reporter, 6,* No.2.

Terman, L. (1916). *The measurement of intelligence: an explanation of and a complete guide for the use of the Stanford revision and extension of the Binet-Simon intelligence scale.* Boston: Houghton Mifflin.

Waddell, K. & Cahoon, D. (1970). Comments on the use of the ITPA with culturally deprived children in the rural south. *Perceptual and Motor Skills, 31.*

Weaver, E. K. (1972). The new literature on the education of the black child. In R. L. Jones (Ed.), *Black Psychology.* New York: Harper and Row.

Wechsler, D. (1944). *The measurement of adult intelligence.* Baltimore: Williams and Wilkins.

Williams, R.L. (1970). Testing and dehumanizing black children. *Clinical Child Psychology Newsletter, a.*

Williams, R.L. (1971). Abuses and misuses in the testing of black children. *The Counseling Psychologist, 2.*

Williams, R.L. (1972, September). The problem of match and mismatch in testing black children. Paper presented to the Annual Meeting of the American Psychological Association, Honolulu, Hawaii.

Williams, R. and Rivers, L. (1975). The effects of language on the test performance of black children, In Robert Williams, (Ed.), *Ebonics: the true language of black folks.* St. Louis: The Institute of Black Studies.

Wolfram, W. (1970). *A socio-lingustic description of Detroit negro speech.* Washington, D.C.: Center for Applied Linguistics.